The British in India: From Trade to Empire

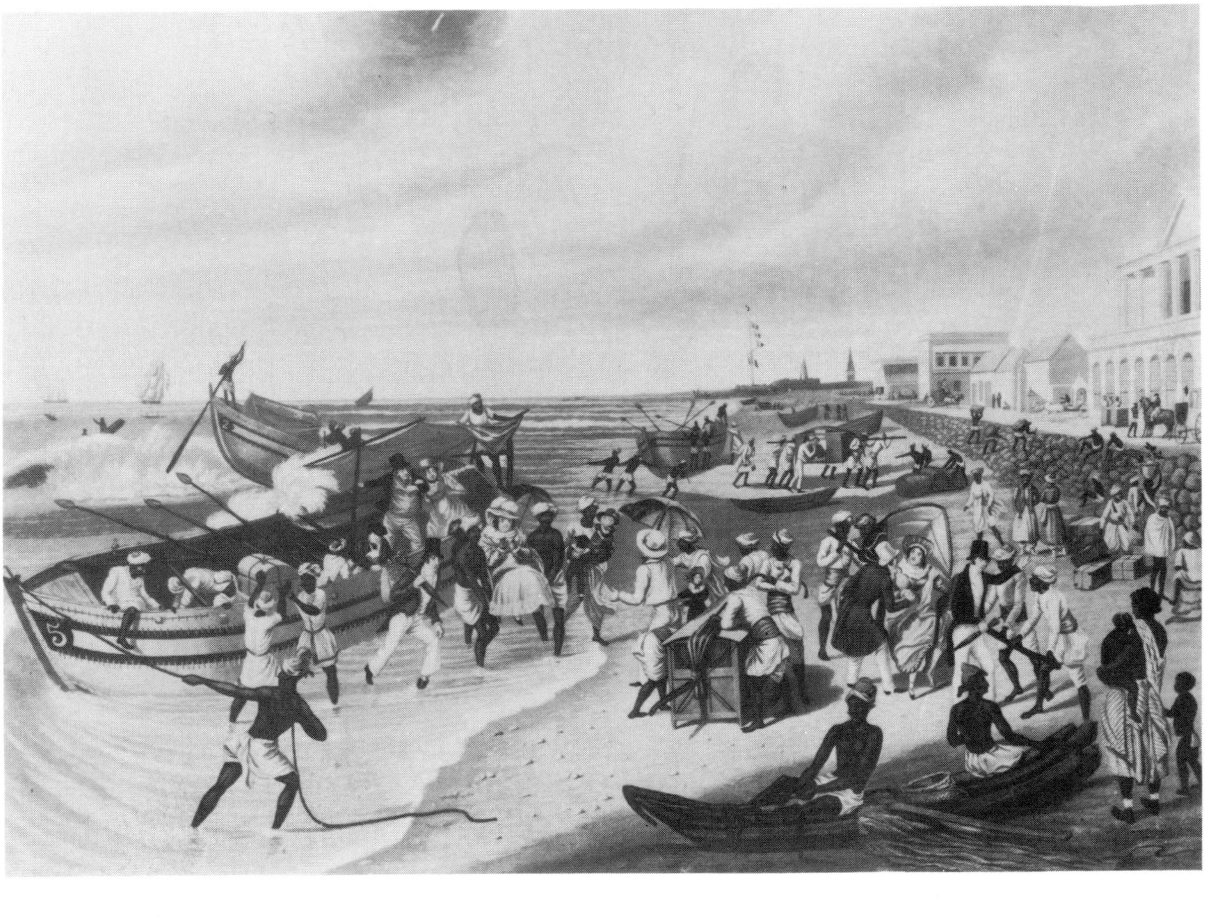

Stephen Ashton

B.T. Batsford Ltd, London

Contents

© Stephen Ashton 1987

First published 1987

Typeset by Tek-Art Ltd, Kent
and printed in Great Britain by
R J Acford Ltd,
Chichester, Sussex
for the publishers
B.T. Batsford Ltd
4 Fitzhardinge Street
London W1H 0AH

ISBN 0 7134 5475 X

Frontispiece
Landing at Madras in massulah *boats.* (India Office Library)

Foreword

Throughout history people have been on the move from one place to another. In this way a large part of the world has become inhabited. For most of human history people moved in small groups, searching for new lands where they could live free from enemies and hunger.

The greatest migration, or movement, of people occurred between 1820 and 1930 and was made possible by the development of the railway and the steam ship. During that period millions of people made the long journey from Europe to America, but also to Australia and New Zealand, and from European Russia eastwards into Siberia. Smaller movements of people also took place in Asia, with Chinese moving into the lands and islands of Southeast Asia and Japanese out into the Pacific and to America.

Most people moved as a result of what can crudely be described as a mixture of "push" and "pull" factors. They were "pushed" out of their homes by poor living conditions, shortage of land, or lack of religious and political freedoms, and "pulled" or attracted to new lands and countries by the hope of a better way of life and new opportunities. For some people migration was largely involuntary: either they did not want to move or they had very little choice. Between 1520 and 1870 millions of Africans were forcibly taken across the Atlantic to America as slaves, and today there are millions of refugees in the world who have been compelled to leave their homes because of war, famine and disease.

Migration mixes people together, not only people from different parts of the same country but also peoples of different languages and cultures. Countries such as the United States and Brazil have been created by people from vastly different backgrounds. And if we look closely at the history of Britain we will see that our language and culture have been shaped by migrants coming to these islands during the last thousand years or more. Migration from Europe to the new lands after 1700 led to the spread of languages (English and Spanish to the Americas, for example), the development of new accents and new cultures, or ways of life.

The aim of this series of books is to look at different examples of "peoples on the move" – why did they leave their original homes? How did they travel? What did they take with them? What did they find in the new lands? How did they settle down? What were relations like between "natives" and newcomers? And what was the impact of new economic systems on the land?

If you have had the experience of moving home, perhaps from one country to another, or even from one place to another *within* a country, then you may be able to share the feelings of people who migrated in the past. If you have never moved home then perhaps these books will help you to understand the reasons why people move, and why in the world today there are, for example, people of European origin living in America and South Africa, and people of African and Asian origin living also in America and in Britain.

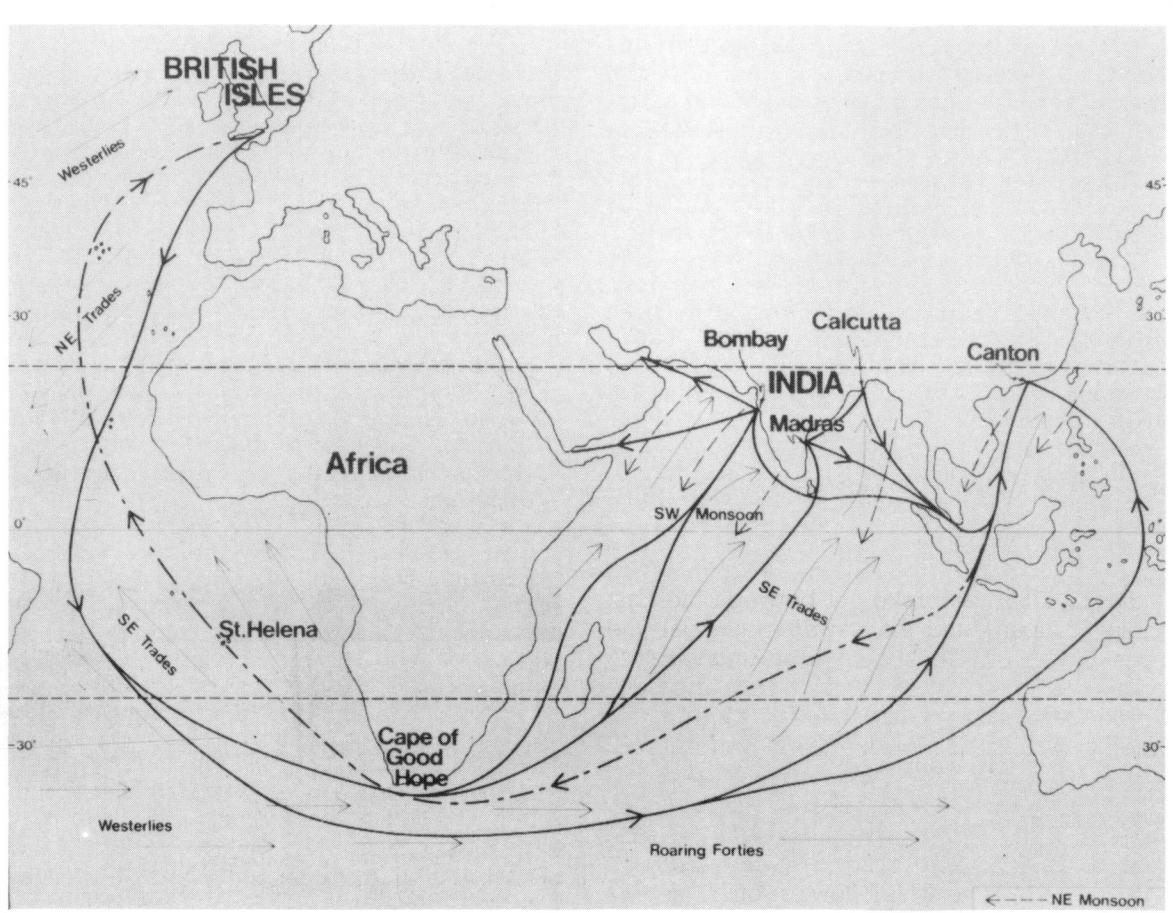

Routes to India.

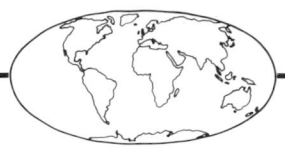

1 Warren Hastings (1732-1818), the First British Governor-General of India

In 1750 a young Englishman by the name of Warren Hastings arrived in Bengal as a writer, or clerk, with the East India Company. His family had once owned estates in Worcestershire but had fallen on hard times. Hastings had excelled at school, but when the time came for him to go to university his family were unwilling to pay for any further education and he was sent to India instead.

In the early eighteenth century the men employed by the East India Company were little more than merchant adventurers. The problem of communication and the ever-changing political situation in India made it very difficult for the men who ran the Company in London to exercise effective control over their employees. Warren Hastings became part of this community of merchants and worked his way through the ranks. In the process he experienced the uncertainty and some of the dangers of life in India. In 1756 war broke out between the East India Company and the *nawab* of Bengal, the ruler of one of India's wealthiest kingdoms, or provinces. The *nawab* had issued an order forbidding the Europeans in Bengal to fortify their trading settlements. When the English refused, the *nawab's* army attacked and captured the English settlement at Calcutta. Hastings was taken prisoner during the attack but he was released unharmed and he managed to secure the release of some of his fellow prisoners. In 1757 an East India Company army under the command of Robert Clive defeated the *nawab's* army at the battle of Plassey. The victory gave the Company effective control of Bengal. The *nawab* was deposed and a new one installed in his place as a figurehead. Hastings was posted as Resident at the Court of the new *nawab*, an appointment which gave him valuable experience of Indian diplomacy.

The men who worked for the East India Company in India were allowed to engage in private trade. Hastings made a modest fortune by this means and returned to Britain in 1764. He squandered most of his money on generous gifts

Warren Hastings, Governor-General of India 1774-85.

to relatives and he was forced through financial hardship to seek re-employment with the East India Company.

When Hastings arrived back in India in 1769 he was appointed second-in-command of the Company's settlement at Madras. In 1772 he became Governor of Bengal and two years later he was made the first Governor-General of British India. Building on the work of men who had gone before him like Robert Clive, Hastings continued the process whereby the East India Company ceased to be an armed trading power and became, instead, a major political and military force. The achievement was remarkable in many ways. The American War of Independence was being fought against Britain on the other side of the world, and in Europe Britain faced a hostile coalition of powers. The government in London was therefore unable to give Hastings much support, but he still managed to defend the Company's possessions in India when they were threatened by powerful Indian kingdoms and the armed forces of the rival French trading company. Hastings' governorship was not all wars and diplomacy. He was responsible for a number of administrative reforms in Bengal, particularly in the collection of land revenue, and he was also an active patron of Western learning about the laws, culture and religions of India.

But Hastings had his enemies, both in India and in Britain. When he was appointed Governor-General in 1774 he was given a four-man Council upon which he had a casting vote. Three of his councillors were appointed from London and one of them, Philip Francis, thought that he would make a better Governor-General than Hastings. The two men became bitter enemies and Francis manipulated the other Council members to ensure that Hastings could not use his casting vote. The experience soured Hastings' character and he became secretive and suspicious. He also became ruthless, resorting to heavy-handed methods to get his own way. He bullied some defenceless members of the Indian nobility into providing him with the money with which to fight the Company's wars. He made enemies with certain members of the Indian merchant community. In 1775 an Indian merchant named Nand Kumar accused Hastings of bribery. The matter was still unresolved when Nand Kumar himself was accused of forgery by another Indian merchant. Nand Kumar was brought to trial,

---

The Impeachment of Warren Hastings

I impeach him [Hastings] in the name of the people of India, whose rights he has trodden under foot, and whose country he has turned into a desert. Lastly, in the name of human nature itself, in the name of both sexes, in the name of every age, in the name of every rank, I impeach the common enemy and oppressor of all.

(Edmund Burke, one of the most formidable political figures of the day, to the House of Lords in 1788 at the opening of Warren Hastings' trial)

Cartoon illustrating the impeachment of Warren Hastings. The noose around Hastings' neck is a symbolic reference to the execution of Nand Kumar. Hastings' accusers in London described the execution as "legal murder".

---

found guilty and executed. Although it was never proved, many at the time suspected that Hastings had influenced the court to condemn Nand Kumar in order to save his own political career.

Hastings was favourably received when he returned to Britain in 1785. He was now a man of substantial means and the money he had made in India enabled him to buy back the estate once owned by his family in Worcestershire. But the atmosphere soon changed. Opinion in Britain was becoming increasingly critical of the activities of the East India Company's servants in India. Bribery and corruption in India were indeed commonplace. Men made fantastic fortunes for themselves but the Company was actually losing money. Hastings became the scapegoat and Philip Francis, his old enemy, gathered support to attack him. In 1788, Hastings faced the humiliation of impeachment – the trial of a public figure for offences committed when holding high office. Initially, the trial attracted enormous interest, to the extent almost that political loyalties in Britain seemed dependent on whether people were for or against Hastings. Interest gradually waned but the trial dragged on for an incredible seven years before Hastings was finally acquitted. The cost of defending himself almost ruined him financially. At stake in the trial was not so much the conduct of one man as the manner in which the British generally conducted their affairs in India. An important principle had at least been established. The days when the Company's servants in India were little more than merchant adventurers were not yet over but they were clearly numbered. Steps were now taken to bring these servants under the control and supervision of Parliament.

The life of Warren Hastings, from the time he first went to India as a young writer with the East India Company, to his being taken prisoner by the troops of an Indian ruler, his governorship first of Bengal and then of India, and finally his impeachment in Britain, is in many ways the story of how the British presence in India took root in the eighteenth century and then established itself on a basis which lasted until India regained its independence in 1947.

The Plunder of Bengal

The five years after Clive's departure may rightly be described as the period of open and unashamed plunder, which took twenty years of effort, both in Britain and on the spot, to correct.... Private trade to the neglect of both Company business and the public service was the main concern.... The beneficiaries of this system were the Company's servants and their Indian agents.... The losers were the merchants and people of Bengal and the Company. The merchants (unattached to the Company) were ruined by unfair competition of men exempt from duty and part of government. The people, whether weavers or agriculturalists, were squeezed both by their Indian rulers and the agents of the Europeans.... The Company suffered because its interests were subordinate to the private ambitions of its own servants, and the exhaustion of the countryside reduced the value of the 'investment' for the export to India.

(Percival Spear, *India: A Modern History*, Ann Arbor, University of Michigan Press, 1961, pp. 199-200)

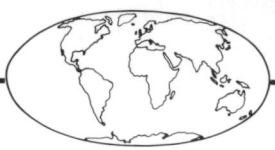

2 The East India Company

In the summer of 1592 a Portuguese galleon, the *Madre de Deus*, dropped anchor at Dartmouth on the south coast of England. The galleon had been captured by English ships off the Azores on her return voyage from the East Indies. The arrival of the *Madre de Deus* caused a sensation. Weighing 1600 tons, 165 feet in length, with seven decks and 32 enormous brass guns, she was the biggest ship that anyone in England had seen. But it was not the size of the ship that caused the excitement. The holds of the ship were crammed with coins, jewels, ivory, silks, calicoes and a variety of spices which included 425 tons of pepper, 45 tons of cloves and 35 tons of cinnamon. The ship's cargo had already been looted by the sailors of the English ships which had attacked and boarded her. The free-for-all continued at Dartmouth, local fishermen ferrying greedy customers out from the quayside. What was left was ferried to London in six freighters. The original cargo was valued at £½ million, nearly half the money in the exchequer of Elizabeth I. The salvaged cargo, with an estimated value of £140,000, was more than enough to whet the appetites of the London merchants, who cast an envious eye over the Portuguese monopoly of trade with the East Indies.

In September 1599 a group of London merchants banded together to raise money for a voyage to the East Indies. They raised £30,133.3s.8d. in subscriptions, but Elizabeth rejected their application for a trading charter because peace negotiations were being conducted with Spain, to which country Portugal was then joined. In the following year, by which time the negotiations had broken down, the merchants tried again with a subscription which was more than double the size of the first. This time, Elizabeth was prepared to agree. On 31 December 1600 she granted a charter to "the Governor and Company of merchants trading to the East Indies". This was the beginning of the East India Company.

The first voyage by a fleet of ships chartered by the East India Company set sail in 1601. Their

List, dated 22 September 1599, of London merchants with their subscriptions to finance a voyage to the East Indies. A second application for a trading charter was granted by Queen Elizabeth I on the last day of 1600.

destination was not India but the spice islands of the East Indies, present-day Indonesia. Spices, of the kind found on the *Madre de Deus*, were in great demand in Europe for a very simple reason: meat went off quickly in the warm summer months; spices not only preserved the meat but also improved its taste by acting as a flavouring. The Company's first voyage was a success. The ships brought back over a million pounds (in weight) of pepper, the sale of which showed a 95 per cent profit for the subscribers. But the Company was unable to establish a foothold in the

East Indies because of European competitors. The power of the Portuguese was beginning to decline but that of the Dutch was on the increase. A Dutch United East India Company was established in 1602, with an investment of £540,000 and an enormous fighting fleet to protect the spice trade. Thwarted in the East Indies, the English East India Company turned its attention to India.

India, too, had spices, but textiles were the main trading attraction, particularly cotton and silk. Indian textiles, especially the painted and

An Indian cloth merchant in his shop selling chintz *to a customer, by an Indian artist, c. 1800. The British admired* chintzes *for their texture and vivid colours. It is hard to imagine what fabric design in the West would have been like without them.*

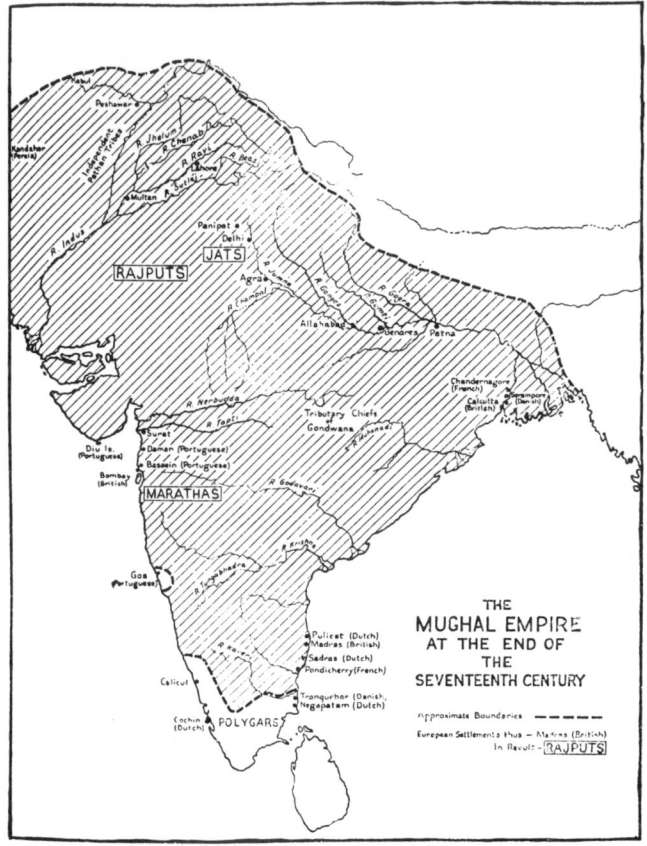

THE MUGHAL EMPIRE AT THE END OF THE SEVENTEENTH CENTURY

Approximate Boundaries ―――――
European Settlements thus ― Madras (British)
In Revolt ― RAJPUTS

◁ *The Mughal Empire at the end of the seventeenth century.*

Mughal splendour: The Taj Mahal at Agra, by an ▷ *Indian artist, c. 1808. The Taj Mahal was built by Emperor Shah Jahan (1628-58) as a tomb for his wife, Mumtaz Mahal.*

and 1530, was descended from Chingis Khan and Tamurlane, the Mongol warlords of Central Asia in the thirteenth and fourteenth centuries. The Mughal Empire was originally only the latest in a line of Muslim empires which had ruled in northern India since the eleventh century. By the end of the seventeenth century, however, the Mughal Empire governed virtually the entire subcontinent. Its size, wealth and power dazzled a succession of European travellers. England, by comparison, seemed but a small principality. The armies of the empire were twice the size of those in Europe. So too were its cities. Painting and architecture, science and literature, flourished under the patronage of the Mughal emperors. Under Akbar, acknowledged as the greatest of the Mughals, who ruled between 1556 and 1605, the land revenue alone of the empire was worth about £15 million. The total revenue of James I of England, Elizabeth's successor, was only £½ million. Mughal India was superior to Europe in other ways. In Europe, kings and princes imposed their own religious beliefs on their subjects. They knew no other way of ensuring their loyalty. Heretics were burnt at the stake, Jews were expelled and long, bloody wars were fought over religion. In India, under Akbar, it was different. Akbar practised and preached religious toleration. He married a Hindu princess and employed Rajputs, Hindu warriors, in his imperial service as governors and military commanders.

Ralph Fitch, an Elizabethan traveller, was the first recorded Englishman to visit India in the 1580s and to see for himself the splendours of Agra and Fatepore, two cities at which Akbar held court. But the first mission to the Mughal Court on behalf of the East India Company was led in 1608 by William Hawkins, a merchant sea-captain. Hawkins carried with him letters from James I to Jehangir, Akbar's successor, requesting permission to establish a factory – a warehouse for storing goods. Impressing Jehangir by his ability to speak Turkish, Hawkins was given a position within the imperial service

run-resist dyed cottons known as *chintzes*, were far superior to the dyed fabrics then produced in Europe. They were admired by the English for their clear colours and for the fact that they could withstand repeated washing. Traditional Indian patterns were somewhat alien to European tastes. In the eighteenth century, therefore, samples of Western patterns were sent out to be copied by Indian artists. The finished products, a mixture of Indian and European design, were used as bedspreads, wall-hangings and dress materials. In addition, India had indigo, a blue dye; saltpetre, used in the manufacture of gunpowder; rice and sugar cane. It also had opium, which was exported to China in return for tea. Huge quantities of tea were sent back to England in the eighteenth century and tea-drinking became established as part of the British way of life.

At the beginning of the seventeenth century, when the East India Company was established, India was the land of the Great Mughals. Mughal was the Persian word for Mongol, and Babur, the first Mughal Emperor, who ruled between 1526 and

The Mughal Empire

Ralph Fitch on the splendours of Agra and Fatepore during the reign of Akbar (1556-1605):

> The king hath in Agra and Fatepore as they doe credibly report 1000 elephants, thirtie thousand horses, 1400 tame Deere, 800 concubines ... Agra and Fatepore are two very great cities, either of them much greater than London and very populous ... Hither is great resort of merchants from Persia and out of India, and very much merchandise of silke and cloth, and of precious stones, both Rubies, Diamonds and Pearles.

(J. Horton Ryley, *Ralph Fitch: England's Pioneer to India and Burma*, Hakluyt Society, London, 1899, pp. 97-9)

Sir Thomas Roe on the extent of the empire during the reign of Jehangir (1605-27):

> His Territorie is farre greater than the Persians, and almost equall, if not as great as, the Turkes. His meanes of money, by revenue, custome of Presents, and inheriting all mens goods, above both. His Countrey lyeth West to Sinde, and so stretcheth to Candahar, and to the Mountaines of Taurus North; to the East as farre as the utmost parts of Bengala, and the borders of the Ganges; and South to Decan. It is two thousand square miles at the least, but hath many pettie Kings within, that are Tributaries.

(William Foster, *The Embassy of Sir Thomas Roe to the Court of the Great Mogul 1615-1619*, Vol. I, Hakluyt Society, London, 1926, p. 111)

and persuaded to take an Indian wife. He stayed in India until 1611 but he was unable to gain permission to establish a factory. He was followed in 1615 by Sir Thomas Roe, a nobleman who acted as James I's ambassador. Roe had been instructed to negotiate a treaty with Jehangir which would grant the English permission to trade at any port within the Mughal Empire. He did not succeed. Instead he had to be satisfied with an imperial edict which granted a number of trading concessions. However, the concessions now included the right to establish factories.

Part of the Charter of King Charles II, dated 27 March 1688, granting the island of Bombay to the East India Company in return for an annual rent of £10.

Throughout the seventeenth century, the East India Company established a small cluster of factories on the Indian coasts. On the west coast, factories were established at Surat and Bombay. (Bombay formed part of the dowry of Catherine de Braganza of Portugal in 1660 when she married Charles II of England.) On the east coast, Fort St George at Madras emerged as the main British settlement. Further north, in Bengal, Fort William was established at Calcutta in 1696.

At the beginning of the eighteenth century the East India Company was still confined to these coastal settlements and the number of Company servants living and working in India was scarcely

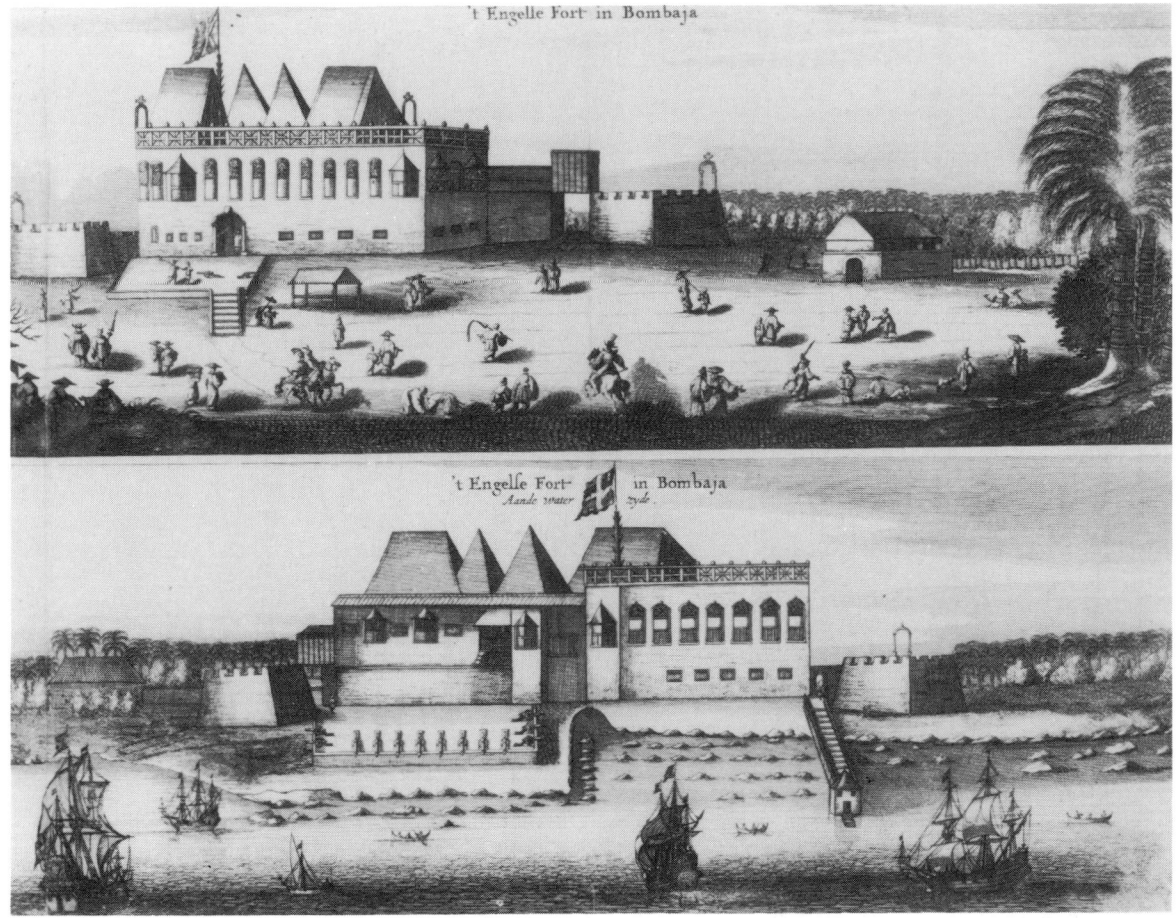

The English factory at Bombay in the early eighteenth century.

more than a few hundred. Aurangzeb, who ruled between 1658 and 1707 and who was the last of the Mughals to be known as "Great", was still on the throne. The British were not the only European power with trading interests in India. The French, Danes, Dutch and Portuguese also occupied small coastal settlements. By the beginning of the nineteenth century, however, the position had been radically transformed. The Mughal Empire was but a shadow of its former self and the East India Company, while not in possession of the entire subcontinent, had emerged as the strongest political power in India.

The reasons for this transformation are many and complex. In a sense, like Rome and a succession of empires before it, the Mughal Empire sowed the seeds of its own decline. Under Aurangzeb, a devout and orthodox Muslim, Akbar's policy of religious toleration and

his partnership with the Hindus came to an end. Under a stricter religious climate the Hindus became the victims of discrimination. In certain areas they responded by launching rebellions. Aurangzeb also pushed forward the boundaries of the empire, particularly in the south, but the newly conquered territories were poor and thus unable to pay for the cost of waging war. At the same time, in western India, a new Hindu power, the Marathas, began to harass the empire on one of its more vulnerable flanks. Aurangzeb was followed by a succession of lesser emperors, under whose weak rule the empire began to fragment. Provincial governors broke away from the centre, asserted their independence and then fought amongst each other to carve out still more territory for themselves. The empire was also dealt mortal blows from outside. The Persians swooped on Delhi, the new Mughal

13

capital, in 1738-9 and the Afghans did the same in 1756-7. Neither power remained to make good their gains, though the Afghans halted the rise of the Marathas, who saw themselves as heirs to the Mughal Empire, by defeating them at the battle of Panipat in 1761.

The politics of mid-eighteenth-century Europe made it possible for European powers to exploit the turmoil in India. Britain and France in particular were rivals in Europe, fighting on opposite sides during the War of the Austrian Succession (1740-8) and again during the Seven Years War (1756-63). Their rivalry was extended to India where they both had trading interests. Britain and France sent out troops, which were used not only in fighting each other but also to tip the scales in the power struggles being fought out between rival Indian rulers. In the long term, sea-power enabled the British to defeat French ambitions in India. Against Indian powers, the lack of unity amongst their opponents enabled the British to gain the upper hand. In 1756 Siraj-ud-daula, the *nawab*, or governor, of Bengal attacked and sacked the poorly defended British settlement at Fort William in Calcutta. Robert Clive, who had already established a reputation as a military leader against the French in south India, was sent north to rescue the British position in Bengal. This he did at the battle of Plassey in 1757 and his victory proved to be a major turning point. Plassey gave the British mastery of Bengal, one of India's richest provinces. The revenues of Bengal enabled the British to muster the forces to fend off the Marathas and then to overcome resistance offered in south India by Haidar Ali, the ruler of the state of Mysore, and his son, Tipu Sultan. All the while a Mughal Emperor sat on the throne at Delhi but he exercised authority in name only. Real power had passed to the East India Company.

It is important to realize that territorial expansion in India was never the objective of the men who managed the affairs of the East India Company in London. Uninterrupted trade was what the men in London wanted. But in an age when the electric telegraph had yet to be invented, it could take anywhere between six and 12 months for communications to travel

Robert Clive (1725-74)

The son of a Shropshire squire, Robert Clive left England to become a writer at Madras in 1743 at the age of 18. He fell overboard on the voyage to India and was rescued by the captain of his ship who threw him a bucket on a rope. He volunteered for military service soon after his arrival in India and much of his life was spent in wars against the rival French trading company and their Indian allies. He played a major role in the transformation of the East India Company from a trading into a territorial power. He amassed a personal fortune in India and was twice Governor of Bengal. He suffered from bouts of depression throughout his life and committed suicide in 1774.

Robert Clive, under whose influence the East India Company was transformed from a trading into a territorial power. He left India for the last time in 1767 and was questioned by a parliamentary committee in 1772 about corruption and mismanagement. "By God", he declared, "at this moment do I stand astonished at my own moderation".

Tipu Sultan – The Tiger of Mysore

Tipu Sultan succeeded his father, Haidar Ali, as *rajah* of the mountainous southern Indian state of Mysore in 1782. He continued his father's policy of opposition to the territorial designs of the East India Company. Tipu had made a model of a tiger mauling a British soldier. The body of the tiger concealed an organ mechanism. When the handle was turned, the organ emitted the roar of a tiger and the shriek of the soldier. The tiger was designed to amuse Tipu and to show what he would like to see happen to the Company's servants. Tipu was killed in action in 1799 when British forces captured his fortress stronghold of Seringapatam. The tiger, captured at the same time, is now kept at the Victoria and Albert Museum in London.

Tipu Sultan, the Tiger of Mysore. By the time of his death in 1799, Tipu's exploits had captured the popular imagination in Britain. References to him in art, literature and drama can be found well into the nineteenth century.

Tipu's Tiger, which can now be seen in the Victoria and Albert Museum in London.

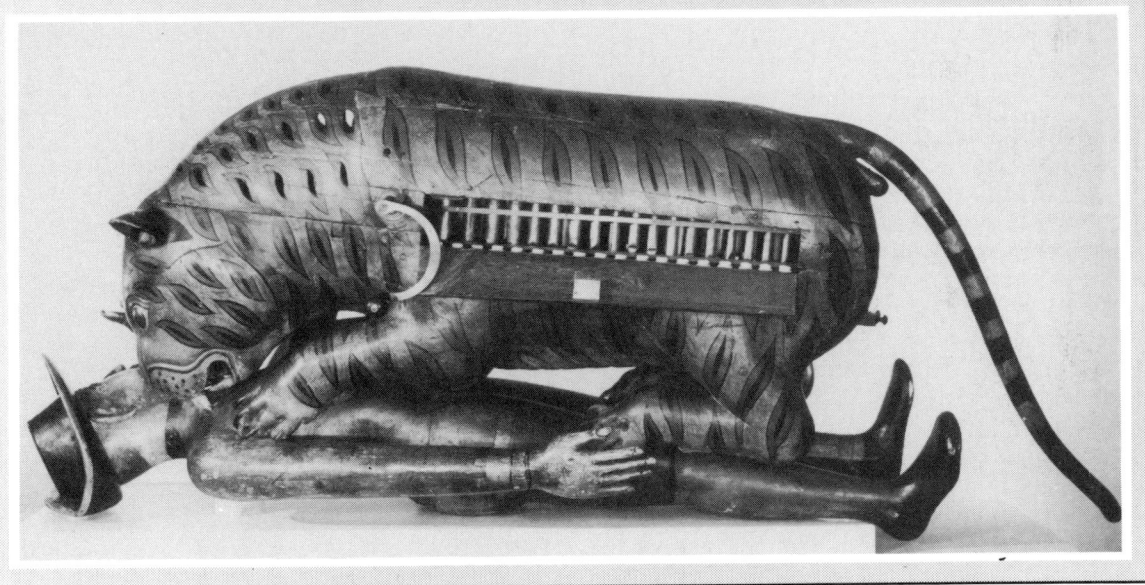

between London and India. The initiative in India, therefore, rested with the British men on the spot, and at times they were a law unto themselves, responding to crises and opportunities as best they saw fit. There was certainly nothing planned about the growth of British power in India.

It is equally important to realize that the British did not go to India as a settler population. Those who travelled knew they would be away many years. But they still regarded Britain as home. They were not trying to cut themselves off by starting a new life in India. Not until the mid-

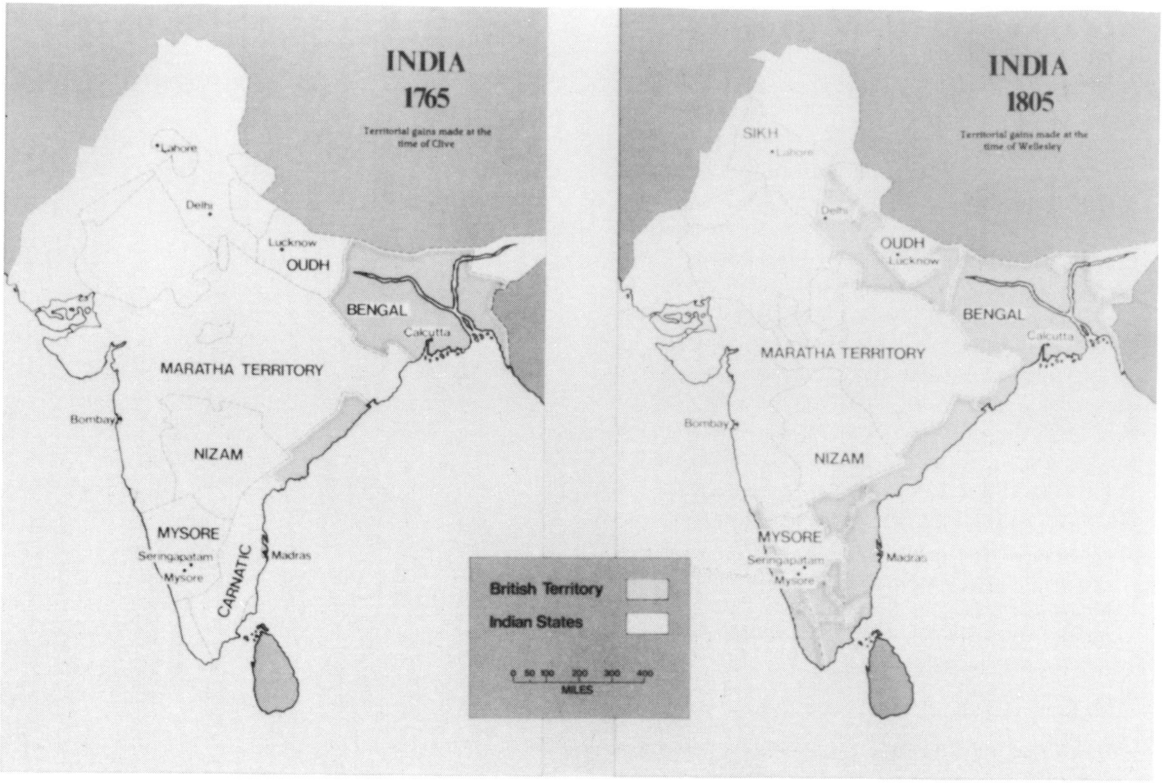

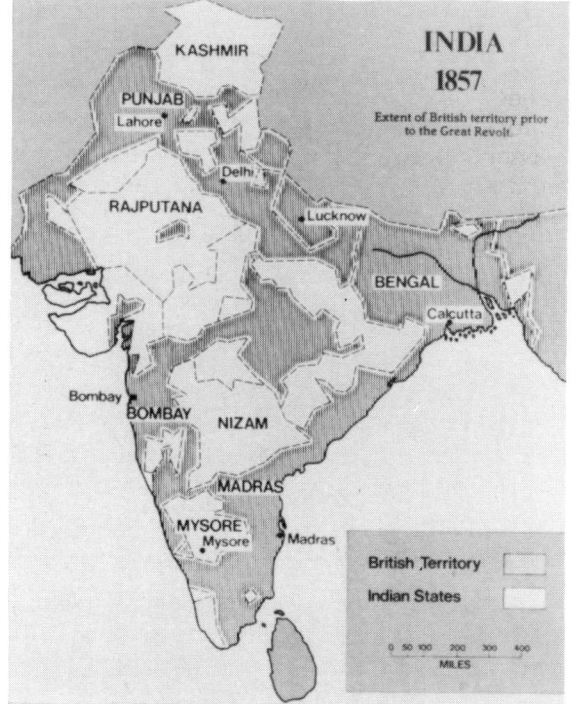

The growth of British territorial power in India: 1765, 1805 and 1857.

nineteenth century did an expatriate community of British mill, factory and plantation-owners emerge in India, and even then it was very small. In the early days most people who went out to India were motivated by a single ambition: to return to Britain as soon as possible once they had made a fortune. This book is about the British in India during the time of the East India Company. It concentrates on the eighteenth century but takes the story forward in chapter seven to the rebellion of 1857, as a result of which the Company was abolished and the Crown took over direct responsiblity for the government of India. The book is not about the growth of British political and military power. Rather, it is about the people who went to India: how they travelled, who they were, the work they did, the domestic and social lives they lived, the views which they formed of Indian people and Indian society, and the impact that they made on India and that India made on them.

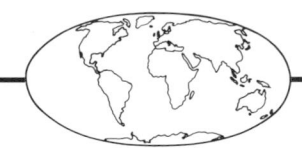

3 A Passage to India

A voyage to India in the eighteenth century could be full of danger. Ships might be attacked by pirates or by enemy powers, such as the French with whom Britain seemed to be constantly at war. Mountainous seas and gales were another hazard. At a time when navigational aids were still rather elementary, ships were lost when they hit rocks or when they ran aground and broke up. Between the years 1700 and 1818, no less than 160 East Indiamen, the sailing ships chartered by the East India Company, were lost by burning, capture or wreck. Some foundered on the treacherous Cornish and Dorset coasts. Their cargoes were worth tens of thousands of pounds. Conditions on board ship, particularly for the ordinary seamen, were appalling. Unsuitable food and drink led to scurvy and the "bloody flux" (dysentery) which, according to Edward Barlow, a seaman who served in eight of the Company's ships between 1669 and 1703, "is seldom cured and killeth a lusty, strong man in ten days". Significant evidence of loss of life is provided by the Burial Registers of St John's Church, Calcutta. The entries between April 1783 and October 1788 contain the names of three captains, 12 officers, two pursers, four surgeons, three surgeon's mates, ten midshipmen, four boatswains, and 80 seamen of all categories below and including the rank of gunner – and this did not include deaths among the passengers. Many, of course, survived the voyage and some – those who could afford it – travelled in relative

The Wreck of the Grosvenor

The *Grosvenor*, an East Indiaman of 729 tons under the command of Captain John Coxon, called at Madras in April 1782 on her way to Europe from Calcutta. She was full with passengers and many prominent members of Bengal society were on board. Her cargo included a small but valuable quantity of diamonds. For safety reasons East Indiamen usually sailed in convoy but the *Grosvenor* set out alone because her two companion ships had been delayed.

Disaster struck the *Grosvenor* in stormy weather during the early hours of Sunday, 4 August 1782, some 500 miles from the Cape of Good Hope on the African coast. Coxon's navigational charts indicated that his ship was at least 300 miles from the nearest land. But the charts were inaccurate and the *Grosvenor* was much nearer to land than he realized. Flickering lights in the distance were assumed at first to be something similar to the Northern Lights. They were, in fact, caused by the fires of burning grass which had been started about 50 miles inland. Panic broke out on the *Grosvenor* when she hit a submerged rock with such force that the masts seemed about to topple over.

As dawn broke Coxon attempted to refloat his ship but she began shipping water. With angry surf breaking over the ship it seemed impossible to get ashore. Two Italian passengers volunteered to swim through the surf to fix a line to the shore. One drowned in the process but the other succeeded. Eventually, 123 people, including the women and children, managed to get ashore. They began to trek to what they thought would be the nearest Dutch settlement, estimating it would take them 17 days. Nearly six months later six seamen stumbled into a settlement about 300 miles from the Cape. A search found ten more sailors and two passengers. None of the others were ever heard of again.

In later years, a *Grosvenor* legend emerged, and the ship's small cargo of diamonds became a fortune in diamonds, sapphires, emeralds, rubies, and gold and silver bars.

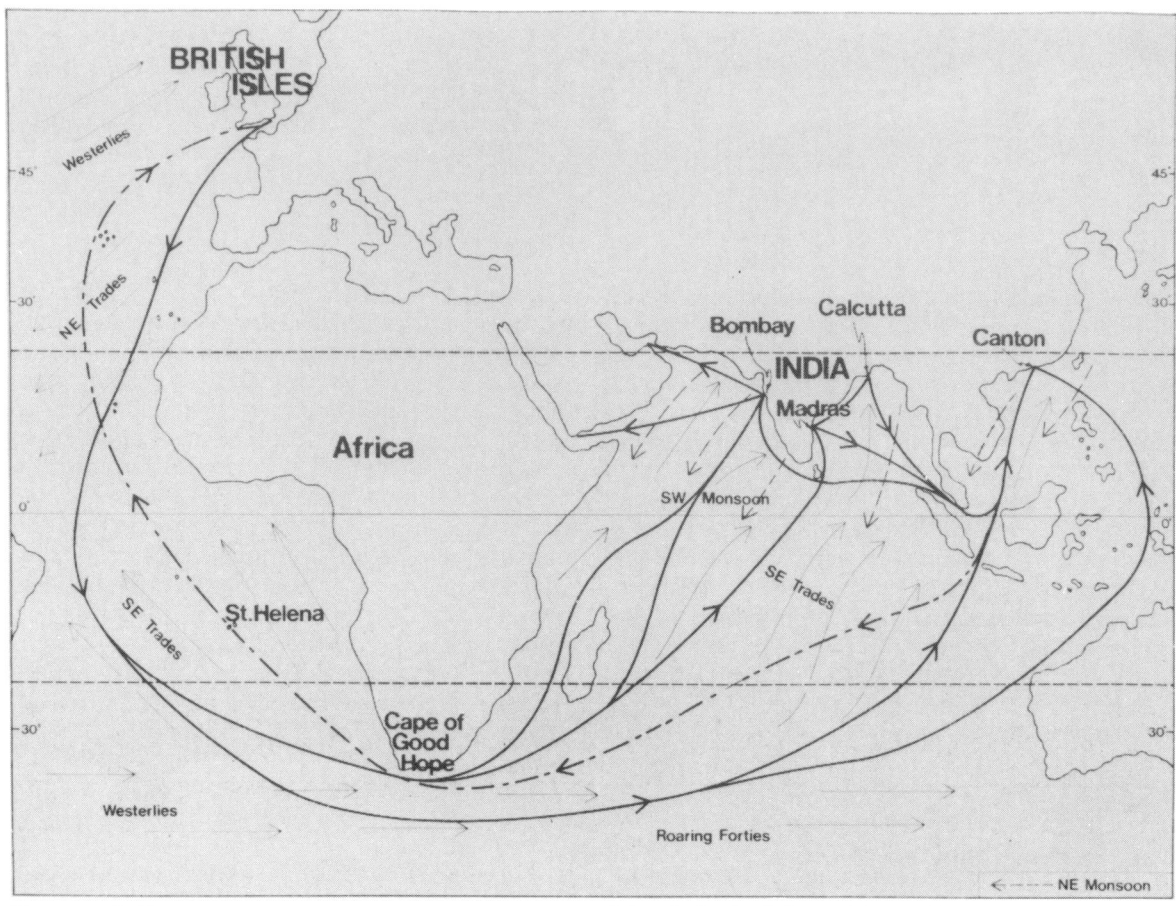

Routes to India.

luxury. Few, however, could have set sail from England without some feelings of apprehension.

Travellers to India·were lucky if they sighted Fort St George at Madras in under four months from the day of sailing from England. The voyage could easily take six months or eight; and when Robert Clive set sail for India for the first time in 1743 he was over a year on the voyage. Voyages to India were determined by the time of year and the prevailing trade winds. One of two routes was taken. The first, and most common, was the coastal route. This dated from the days of coastal navigation when ships never ventured more than a few days' sailing from the nearest land. After crossing the Bay of Biscay, ships put in at Madeira to pick up supplies of fresh meat and vegetables and plentiful stocks of Madeira wine, which was in great demand among Europeans in India. They then sailed down the west coast of Africa, round the Cape of Good Hope and stopped again to pick up supplies at one of the numerous Comoro

Islands in the Mozambique Channel. Finally, they made their way across the Indian Ocean, their destinations being one of the British settlements at Calcutta, Bombay or Madras. The second route took the same course to Madeira but then crossed the Atlantic to Brazil, which was then under Portuguese rule. After stopping for supplies at Rio de Janeiro, ships then sailed due south to catch the Roaring Forties, the trade winds at 40 degrees latitude which enabled ships to bypass the Cape of Good Hope and make their way at great speed up into the Indian Ocean, or, if they were destined for Canton in China, into the South China Sea.

To become the captain of an East Indiaman, a man had to be 25 years of age and to have made at least one voyage to and from either India or China as either chief or first officer. On board, the authority of the captain was absolute and his privileges were extensive. Each officer was allowed a certain amount of space in the hold which he filled with his own merchandise, carried out, as the phrase went, "on his privilege". The amount of space was determined by the rank

The captains of East Indiamen often illustrated their logs with diagrams and sketches. This sketch was drawn by William Wilson, captain of the Suffolk, *during a return voyage to China, October 1755 to September 1757.*

Discipline on Board an East Indiaman

In December 1787 the crew of the *Belvedere* mutinied off the coast of China. Every officer down to the midshipman was thrown overboard but none drowned. The ringleaders were caught. The log of the *Belvedere*, dated 24 December 1787, records how they were punished:

At seven a.m., having unrigged the long boat, made a stage on her and sent her on board the Commodore for to have Berry and Lilly flogged round the fleet, which was done accordingly – round eighteen ships. At noon the captain brought Lieff, Ladson, Jackson, Skinner, Langford, Connor and Hastings on board from the *Earl Fitzwilliam* to receive their punishment: when Kieff and Ladson had five dozen lashes each, Connor, Jackson and Skinner four dozen, and Langford and Hastings two dozen.

(India Office Records)

---

of the officer and so the captain had the lion's share. On the outward voyage he took hats and shoes, perfumes and glassware, clocks and silverware, Madeira and claret, cutlery and crockery , hams and pickles. By this means the shops of Calcutta, Bombay and Madras were kept stocked with European goods. On the return journey, the hold would be filled with all manner of privilege goods and it was not unknown for a captain to make as much as £30,000 from a two-way voyage. In addition to his earnings from his privilege trade, the captain also charged passage rates to his passengers. Rates were fixed for employees of the East India Company but private passengers had to bargain with the captain. Fees ranged from £200 to £1000, depending on the accommodation being offered.

The Navigation Acts of the seventeenth century laid down that the captain and at least three-quarters of the crew of ships trading in Asia should be British. The crews were recruited in the Thameside area from Wapping to Rotherhithe. Because of the value of a ship's cargo, the crew was expected to be able to defend her as well as sail her. Discipline on board for the ordinary seaman was savage. Floggings and keel-haulings were commonplace. Frequently the crews of East Indiamen were press-ganged into the Royal Navy. More and more men were taken by the Royal Navy towards the end of the eighteenth century because of the Revolutionary Wars against the French. To make good the numbers, the owners of East Indiamen were forced to use increasing numbers of Indian and Chinese seamen who were known as *lascars*. *Lascars* could only be employed on the home voyage; the crew of a ship on the outward voyage had to be predominantly British. *Lascars* were supposed to be taken back as passengers. In between voyages they were lodged in hostels in the Shoreditch area of the East End of London. Conditions were squalid and insanitary. Many never made it back home. Those that did had to work their passage. *Lascars* were treated as little more than slaves.

Depending on the size of a ship's cargo, an average-sized East Indiaman might carry up to 100 passengers. Many of the passengers on an outward voyage would be youngsters going to India for the first time as writers or cadets in the Company's service. Writers were usually aged between 16 and 18, but cadets might be younger still – boys of 14. Both were known as "griffins" (newcomers), a label which they carried with them until they had been in India for a year. As well as some more senior Company servants, a handful of ladies might be found on board. The practice of sending young ladies out to India to find husbands was just coming into fashion although, as we shall see, few were successful. The ladies were usually accompanied by a chaperone. If alone, they were placed under the

Conduct Becoming in a Young Lady
Worried parents issued to their daughters clear instructions on how to behave and how to avoid romantic entanglements during the voyage to India. In 1821 Mr Peter Cherry, a Company servant stationed at Madras, arranged a passage for his three daughters to join him on the East Indiaman *General Harris*. He sent ahead a memorandum explaining how they should behave on board:

> Before I proceed to more serious matters let me add that nothing is so indelicate, indeed so indecent, as from the windows of ladies' cabins to see anything towing overboard or being hung out to dry; neither is anything more severely censured than loud talking, dancing over the heads of those in the great cabin, thus indelicately attracting the attention of persons in the next cabin or cuddy . . .

(*The Annals of an Anglo-Indian Family*, printed privately)

care of the captain. The presence of one or two young ladies on board a shipload of men inevitably turned many heads. The young men competed for their favours and duels were sometimes fought over the attentions of a young woman at the first convenient landing place.

Accommodation on board varied enormously and depended on status and the ability to pay. The most expensive accommodation was in the roundhouse at the stern of the ship. Here most of the cabins had portholes, providing the occupants with light and air. Ladies travelling alone usually had cabins in the roundhouse, partly for privacy and partly so that the captain could keep an eye on them. Immediately forward of the roundhouse cabins was the cuddy. The cuddy was often divided into two spaces, with the captain's stateroom on one side and the dining room on the other. Underneath the roundhouse was the great cabin, which was divided into spaces for bachelor army officers and other gentlemen passengers who could not afford the roundhouse. Forward of the great cabin was the

An interesting scene on board an East Indiaman.

The First Few Moments on Board an East Indiaman

17-year-old Thomas Twining was one of the passengers rowed out to the East Indiaman *Ponsbourne* moored off Deal in Kent in 1792. He recalled his first few minutes on board:

> Having made a bow to the Captain and officers . . . I inquired where my cabin was. I was conducted down a ladder to it, on the lower or gundeck, not far from the stern on the larboard [port] side. Here, the port being shut, there was scarcely light enough for me to survey my new appartment. I soon found, also, that the ship had considerably more motion than was apparent from the boat, and that the relief which I felt in coming on board was of very short duration. For I was scarcely able to stand without laying hold of some fixed object. I also became exceedingly oppressed by a close suffocating air, and by a sickening offensive smell . . . the smell of the ship. My head and stomach began to yield to this irresistible combination. I could hardly help returning to the deck to breathe a little pure air.
>
> (William H.G. Twining, ed., *Thomas Twining: Travels in India a Hundred Years Ago*, James R. Osgood, Mcilvanie & Co., London 1893, p. 5)

ship's steerage, beneath which was a large undivided area normally occupied by writers and cadets. Accommodation here was cramped. Hammocks were slung where space existed. There was no light and hardly any air. The stale atmosphere and the constant lurching roll of the ship caused seasickness. Passengers booked space only on board ship: such furniture as they needed they had to provide themselves.

Basic provisions for the voyage were always a

problem, especially water. It was taken from the Thames in a foul and stinking condition. Some passengers wisely carried "filtering machines" to remove the worst of the pollution and sediment, but even these could not improve the colour or the sickly smell. However, as the voyage progressed, the water's organic content underwent a series of natural chemical changes that left it reasonably clear and sweet. Also, fresh water could always be obtained when the ship stopped to pick up supplies. After water, the hard tack or biscuit was the most important provision, but it was hardly the most popular. William Hickey, a regular traveller to and from India in the eighteenth century, wrote in his memoirs in 1769: "There is nothing I felt the want of so much as bread", the biscuit being "uncommonly hard and flinty". The crew's staple diet of salt beef or pork, equally unpopular, was varied by dried fish, dried peas and beans, cereals, cheese, butter and, later, lemons, the juice of which helped to keep scurvy at bay. Livestock, carried mainly for

the captain's table, led a wretched existence – sheep crowded into the long-boat and poultry in pens on the poop. The captain and the wealthy passengers who dined with him in the cuddy usually ate well. Lady Anne Barnard, travelling out with her husband in 1797, recorded in her diary that the menu for one dinner consisted of pease soup, roast leg of mutton, hogs' puddings, two fowls, two hams, two ducks, corned round of beef, mutton pies, pork pies, stewed cabbage and potatoes, which were followed by an enormous plum pudding washed down with porter, spruce beer, wine, sherry, gin and rum. All this was for sixteen passengers.

For the passengers, the most enjoyable part of the voyage would be when the ship put in at its various ports of call. They could stretch their legs and breathe fresh air after weeks of confinement. On board ship all but the most fortunate had to put up with cramped conditions, unappetizing food and the stench of billage. Entertainment consisted of playing cards, musical evenings and

Fort St George at Madras in the eighteenth century.

simply making conversation. As a precautionary measure against fire and also to avoid detection by enemy ships or by pirates, candles in cabins had to be put out by ten o'clock at the latest in the evening.

Eventually, after months at sea, the passengers would catch their first glimpse of the Indian coast. If destined for Madras, the outline of Fort St George would gradually appear. As the ship drew nearer its guns would begin to salute the fort and tiny puffs of smoke rising from the turrets of the fort would indicate that the fort was returning the greeting. Having dropped anchor, the ship would be surrounded by hundreds of local fishermen in their *massulah* boats, which were made of thin planks sewn together with coconut fibres. Into these the apprehensive passengers would descend. They were rowed through the surf to the edge of the shore – a hair-raising and at times dangerous experience – and then carried on to dry land on the back of a wet and slippery fisherman. A gabble of unfamiliar tongues greeted them. They had arrived in India.

Landing at Madras in massulah *boats. Being rowed ashore in one of these boats was a dangerous experience at times. It was not unknown for people to be drowned.*

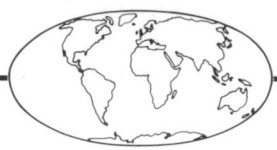

4 The Company's Servants

The headquarters of the East India Company were at Leadenhall Street in the City of London. The governing body was the Court of Directors and the senior members were the Chairman and Deputy Chairman. The Court consisted of 24 directors elected by the Court of Proprietors, who represented the shareholders.

All appointments in the Company's overseas service were made by the Court of Directors. At first the Company employed experienced merchants who had already worked abroad – preferably in Spain, North Africa and the Near East – and who could speak either Portuguese, Turkish or Persian – useful languages in the setting of Mughal India. But by 1668 young men or teenage boys, called "apprentices" or "writers", were also being sent out to India. In that year the

Directors decided that they had enough men of "age, abilities and quallity" in India. In future they intended

> . . . only to send from home young men or youths, to be trayned up in our business, for wee have observed the advantages, that others have by this way, in the knowing and well managdement of affairs, by encouraging young men, in hopes of preferement [promotion], to be sober, industrious and faithfull.
>
> (Directors to Fort St George, 20 November 1668, India Office Records)

By the eighteenth century most of the Company's servants going out to India on their first

East India House, headquarters of the East India Company in Leadenhall Street in the City of London. The Company's Library was founded here in 1801. The unique collection of drawings, prints and manuscript material which was gathered is now preserved within the India Office Library and Records.

appointment were young men with the rank of writer. In 1751 the minimum age was fixed at 16 and the youths had to satisfy the Directors that they had been through "a regular course of arithmetick and merchants' accounts".

As well as appointments on the commercial side, the Directors also made military appointments to the Company's armed forces in India. Initially, these troops were small in number and were employed to provide local protection for the factory or trading settlement. Their numbers grew significantly during the eighteenth century as the East India Company became involved in the intrigues of Indian politics and in wars against the French. Again, as in the case of writers, it became customary to appoint young men as cadets to serve as junior officers in the Company's army. The Directors also appointed chaplains, surgeons, ships' captains, naval officers, port agents, engineers, surveyors and an increasing number of labourers for the extensive Company docks and warehouses. But, without question, the most prestigious appointments were those on the commercial and administrative side. Young men who went out to India as writers became part of what was known as the "covenanted" service. Upon joining, they had to sign a covenant or agreement which bound them to obey the Company's orders. They also had to give two securities of £500 each as guarantees of their good behaviour. The covenanted servants were the men responsible for managing the Company's trade, buying and selling its goods, administering the early settlements and, ultimately, by the end of the eighteenth century, taking over the government of large areas of India.

A series of graded ranks was established in 1706 in a form which was to last for nearly 100 years. A man served as a writer for five years before becoming a factor; three years later he became a junior merchant; and three years later still he reached the highest rank in the service – that of senior merchant. Although there were rewards for exceptional talent, promotion usually went strictly according to seniority. The longest-serving senior merchants became members of the councils which ran the affairs of the Company's settlements in Bengal, Bombay and Madras. The settlements were sometimes known as "presidencies", because each of the councils was headed by a president appointed by the Court of Directors in London. In time, the presidents became known as governors.

Throughout the eighteenth century the centre of British commercial and political activity shifted towards Bengal and the Company's settlement at Fort William in Calcutta assumed increasing importance. By the Regulating Act of 1773 the Governor of Bengal became Governor-General, with supervisory authority over the other governors and councils in Bombay and Madras. The Act came into force the following year and Warren Hastings, who had entered the Company's service as a writer in 1749, became the first Governor-General.

From 1749, writers' petitions – applications for writerships – survive. These petitions provide essential information about the backgrounds of the men who entered the Company's service. Candidates were required to produce certificates giving details of their age and qualifications. They also had to submit testimonials (character references). The petitions indicate that the vast majority of writers

---

Petition of Warren Hastings for a writership with the East India Company, November 1749. It reads: "He therefore humbly prays your Honours will please to entertain him in that Station which he promises to discharge with the greatest Diligence and Fidelity, and is ready to give such Security as your Honours shall require."

came from middle-class commercial or merchant families, with a sprinkling from the clergy and landed aristocracy. Scotsmen, with their reputation as shrewd and successful businessmen, were well represented. Patronage played an important part in East India Company appointments: writers were often the sons or close relatives of the Directors. Connections with the East India Company tended to be hereditary. Men who had served in India sought election to the Court of Directors upon their return to Britain. If successful, they were then in a position to nominate their own sons as writers. East India Company families also frequently intermarried. Several generals of the same family served in India – the Barwells, the Chicheley Plowdens and the Thackerays, into which family William Makepeace Thackeray, the famous nineteenth-century novelist and author of *Vanity Fair*, was born.

There were other, rather more dubious, ways of entering the Company's service. Notices appeared in the London newspapers during the second half of the eighteenth century advertising writerships for as much as £2000 or £3000. Cases of straightforward bribery were not unknown. William Hickey, one of the most colourful British figures in eighteenth-century India, recalled in his memoirs a story involving Colonel Auchmuty. When asked by Lord Cornwallis, the Governor-General, how he had managed to get two of his sons into the civil service and another into the military service of the Company, the Colonel replied:

> By my soule I had many friends there, sure enough, staunch ones too, no fewer than five thousand, my Lord! . . . I gave the lads of Leadenhall Street [the Directors] five thousand guineas for the writerships in Bengal for my two eldest whelps, and so in the generosity of their hearts they threw a cadetship into the bargain for my youngest spalpeen.
>
> (Alfred Spencer, ed., *Memoirs of William Hickey*, Vol. 4, Hurst & Blackett Ltd, London, 1948, pp. 109-10)

Writerships were clearly much in demand. But the attraction was not the nature of the work, and certainly not the salary. Writers were little more than human xerox machines, who spent many tedious hours perched on highstools laboriously copying by hand the despatches and account ledgers which were sent to the Court of Directors in London. At the beginning of the eighteenth century a writer was paid £5 a year, a factor £15, a junior merchant £30, a senior merchant £40, and a governor, who was a special case, £300. Salaries were supplemented by various allowances for food, servants and housing or rent. But only a governor received some sort of living wage, allowances boosting his salaries to about £2300. The others found it impossible to live on their salaries and allowances. The cost of living was expensive. In 1754 Stair Dalrymple, a newly arrived writer, found "everything here . . . double the price it is at home" and estimated that his salary would only pay for six months' living expenses. It was not uncommon for new writers to find themselves heavily in debt.

However, the main attraction of serving with the East India Company was the prospect it offered, in the long term, of making a personal fortune. Company servants, both civil and military, were allowed to engage in private trade on their own account. All trade in goods travelling between Europe and Asia was conducted by the East India Company and no English merchant ship was allowed round either the Cape of Good Hope or Cape Horn unless it belonged to the

---

An Ambitious Young Writer

Stair Dalrymple, a Scotsman, set sail from England in 1752 at the age of 17. On the eve of his departure he wrote a letter to his brother:

> This day, after very long suspense, I am appointed by the Directors of the United East India Company as a Writer in their Settlements in that place . . . I look upon myself now as a man of Business. I don't think a voyage to the East Indies is like the one I made to Norway for five or so weeks. I expect it to be a Duration of fifteen or twenty years at least. In that time I may be made Governour. If not that, I may make a Fortune which will make me live like a Gentleman . . . . We are obliged to serve the Company for the space of five years, for little or nothing recompense. But that don't signifie much for we have the Liberty to Trade as much as we please and at the end of five years we may be great men by good Interest.
>
> (Stair Dalrymple to Sir Hugh Dalrymple, 1 November 1752, Scottish Record Office)

Company. Individuals could only trade with Europe if they were able to persuade a ship's captain to sell them his privilege cargo space for the return voyage, or if they entrusted their goods to foreign ships. But Company servants were given a free hand to take part in the "country trade", that is, trade within India or between India and the surrounding Asian countries. Only two products – calicoes and pepper – were excluded because, again, the Company had a monopoly. Private trade was encouraged because it enabled individuals to make fortunes, cost the Company nothing and turned the English factories into bustling ports from which the Company could collect a large revenue in customs and taxation.

To make the most of private trade, Company servants were heavily dependent on the Indian merchant community. In Bengal these merchants were known as *banians*, in Madras as *dubashes*. Contemporary English opinion of the *banian* and *dubash* was invariably critical. They were portrayed as knaves who made vast fortunes of their own by cheating their English employers. But this prejudice concealed their true value. In a sense, the relationship between a Company official and his *banian* or *dubash* was one of master and servant. New English arrivals in India were usually besieged by *banians* or *dubashes* offering their services. They sometimes found accommodation for the newcomer and subsequently managed his household and his personal spending. But there was much more to the relationship. *Banians* and *dubashes* acted as agents or brokers. Some, like Cantu Babu, *banian* to Warren Hastings, were among the richest and most influential members of the Indian community in Calcutta. Their services were indispensable. They provided the local knowledge and advanced the loans without which the Company servant could neither buy nor sell his goods.

Clive's Indian Fortune

Clive's victory at Plassey in 1757 made the British the masters of Bengal. Thereafter the *nawabs* of Bengal were little more than puppets, their final humiliation coming in 1765 when the Mughal Emperor granted the *diwani* of Bengal – the right to collect the land revenue – to the East India Company. Plassey set off a succession struggle in Bengal. Siraj-ud-daula was deposed and Mir Jafar, the leading contender, installed in his place. But Mir Jafar had to pay an enormous price for British support. The *nawabs* of Bengal were said to be worth £40 million, a wildly exaggerated figure. Nevertheless, Mir Jafar paid out £1,238,575 to secure British backing. All manner of people profited, from members of the Bengal Council to the Company's more senior military and naval officers. Clive, with presents worth £176,000, did the best. His takings did not end there. Mir Jafar obtained for Clive a Mughal title, "Zubdat ul Mulk" (Select of the Kingdom), and the rank of *mansabdar*, one of the highest within the imperial service. To match his new-found status, Clive was given a *jagir*, a land grant, which entitled him to keep the revenue proceeds of a particular district. Clive's *jagir* gave him an annual salary of £30,000. When Clive left India for the last time in 1767 his Indian fortune was worth £401,102. He was twice appointed Governor of Bengal, 1758-60 and 1765-7. Rather ironically, Clive was sent back to Bengal for a second time in 1765 to root out corruption within the administration.

William Watts, Clive's agent, negotiating with Mir Jafar (left), the new nawab of Bengal, and his son, Miran, after the battle of Plassey in 1757.

THE COMPANY'S SERVANTS

Private trade brought enormous profits to some of the Company's servants, sometimes by highly irregular means. Some individuals used the money which they had been given to buy goods on behalf of the Company to finance their own trade. Others sold their own goods to the Company at prices which they fixed themselves. They used Indian names, often those of their *banian* or *dubash*, as a cover.

But the profits from private trade paled into insignificance when compared with the huge sums which were extracted in presents, essentially bribes, from the *nawabs* of Bengal after Clive's victory at the battle of Plassey in 1757. A Select Committee of the House of Commons in London estimated in 1772 that the staggering sum of £2,169,665 had been taken in presents between 1757 and 1765. Clive, who returned from India to become one of the richest men in England, profited the most. It would be wrong to portray every Company servant as corrupt and dishonest. Only a select few benefited from presents. It would be equally wrong to apply present-day moral standards to the eighteenth century. Moreover, for every story of a fortune made there were others which told of men being ruined financially or dying prematurely in India before they had a chance to enjoy their gains. But those who did make money, by fair means or foul, had but one ambition after serving in India: to retire to a life of comfort and ease as a country gentleman in Britain.

Returning Company servants were known as "nabobs", an anglicized version of the Indian *nawab*. A nabob was a man who returned from the East with a fortune. Nabobs were not popular in Britain. They were regarded as social climbers and, because of their wealth, were viewed with a mixture of envy and resentment. The common image of the nabob was of a man who flaunted his wealth, living in a palatial country house and commissioning artists to paint his portrait, often depicting scenes of his exploits in India. Some used their money to buy their way into positions of influence, either as Justices of the Peace or as Members of Parliament. The more eccentric nabobs were the targets of social gossip. They were satirized in cartoons and plays.

Returning nabobs created considerable interest in Britain in the affairs of the East India Company. They seemed to confirm a growing impression that all was not well in India. The Company's wars and the new administrative responsibilities were proving very costly. By the third quarter of the eighteenth century the Company was having to apply to the government for loans to ease its financial difficulties. Loans were granted but they were far from welcome to a government which was faced at the same time by a revolt of its American colonies on the other side of the world. A number of parliamentary enquiries were set up to investigate the affairs of the Company. In 1784, the Company was made answerable to parliament by the establishment of a Board of Control in London. The most spectacular enquiry into the affairs of the Company was the impeachment of Warren Hastings, which was described in Chapter 1.

As a result of reforms introduced towards the end of the eighteenth century, the nature of employment under the East India Company changed significantly. The Company was still a commercial body but more and more men were appointed as administrators. Under Lord Cornwallis, Governor-General between 1786 and 1793, the service was divided into commercial and administrative branches, and new recruits had to opt for one or other. In future, a man could be a merchant or an administrator. He could not be both. Eventually, in the nineteenth century, the whole of the Company's service became administrative. Trade with India was left in private hands.

Cornwallis was responsible for another, equally significant, reform. Previously, the Company had employed Indian officials to administer justice and to collect revenue. Their knowledge of local conditions, customs and languages was invaluable. Cornwallis, however, distrusted Indian officials. "Every native of India", he wrote, "is corrupt". Indian officials were dismissed and in 1793 senior administrative posts were reserved exclusively for Europeans. Cornwallis thought little better of his own people but believed that better salaries would curb the dishonesty and corruption. The means were also close at hand to enable the Company to appoint the right sort of recruit. In 1809 an East India Company College was opened at Haileybury in Hertfordshire. The College became a training school for Company servants. It functioned until the Company was abolished in 1858 at the end of the Great Revolt in India. Thereafter, Indian civil servants were recruited by means of a competitive examination from university graduates.

The nabobs. Lord Cornwallis (the portly figure in the doorway) holding a reception at Government House, Calcutta, in 1792. When they returned to Britain the nabobs were viewed with a mixture of resentment and envy because of the manner in which they often flaunted their new-found wealth.

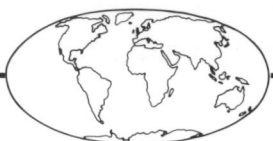

5 Domestic and Social Life

The early East India Company settlements in India were very small. The English civilian population of Fort St George at Madras in 1700 was estimated at 114. A company of soldiers brought the total population to about 400. The civilians included 27 Company servants and 29 freemen. Freemen were free merchants or private traders. In theory, anyone not employed by the East India Company needed a licence from the Court of Directors before they could travel to India. They were obliged to live in the Company's settlements under the authority of a governor and to sign a covenant of good behaviour. In practice, many more individuals went out to India than had licences. They travelled by foreign ships or took the overland route via the Persian Gulf. Some joined the crew of a Company ship and then deserted when they arrived in India.

At Madras, the English lived in Fort St George itself, which was more like a miniature walled town than a fortress. The area inside the walls was only about 400 x 100 yards. The houses were close together. They were tall and spacious and rather Italian-looking, with big shuttered windows and colonnades. The Governor's house was the largest, and there was a hostel for the writers and a barracks for the troops. The other buildings were offices, warehouses and two churches, one Church of England, the other Roman Catholic. Immediately beyond the wall on the north side of Fort St George was what the English described as the "Black Town". It had a population of about 400,000. Portuguese, Armenians and Jews lived there, as well as Indians, giving it a very cosmopolitan appearance. It was a typical Eastern town, the houses close together and the narrow streets bustling with activity. There were all the smells of India – joss sticks burning in the shops, fruit and jasmine, the spicy aroma of cooking food and the smell of burnt dung which was used as fuel.

With numbers so small, life in the early Company settlements bore a strong resemblance to that of an Oxford or Cambridge college, or to that of a great merchant household in London, where the master slept with his family over his place of business, servants and apprentices over them in the attic, and porters and messengers packed away anywhere in the cellars and warehouses. The day began at six with prayers led by the chaplain. The mornings were devoted to business, the writers perched on their stools copying the despatches, the Governor and his senior merchants touring the warehouses or bargaining with local Indian traders. The inhabitants of the settlements met for dinner at noon and for supper at eight at a common table. They were seated according to their rank, with the Governor presiding at the head of the table. With high-spirited writers and cadets in attendance, mealtimes were sometimes boisterous affairs. The Directors wrote to the Council at Fort St George in 1710:

> **We are sorry to hear that of late there has not been sufficient decorum kept up among our people, and particularly among the young writers and factors, and that there have been Files of Musqueteers sent for to keep the peace at dinner time.**
>
> (Quoted in Percival Spear, *The Nabobs*, Oxford University Press, 1932, p. 12.)

Many young Company servants suffered from boredom and homesickness. Robert Clive was frequently depressed during his early years in India. His spirits sank when a ship arrived from England without a letter from his family. "I have not enjoyed one happy day since I left my native country", he wrote to a cousin in England from Fort St George in 1745. "Letters were surely first invented for the comfort of such solitary wretches as myself." There was not much social life. With so little to do, many of the young men lapsed into frequent bouts of drinking and gambling. The gates of the fort were shut at 10 at night and no one was allowed out. At 11 the soldiers patrolled the streets of the Black Town to close the taverns and punch-houses and to round up late-night revellers.

During the second half of the eighteenth

century, as the power of the East India Company increased and the British population expanded, the pattern of domestic life changed considerably. The Company's employees began to move out of the cloistered confines of the early settlements. Calcutta, which was rebuilt after it had been sacked by Siraj-ud-daula in 1756, grew up as an English town. By 1800 it had a population of just under 200,000. The non-official European community – that is, those not employed by the East India Company – was estimated at about a thousand. A list drawn up in 1793 gives an idea of some of their occupations: 12 teachers, 11 surgeons, 2 portrait painters, 2 architects, 4 hairdressers, 3 jewellers, 12 tailors, 25 cabinetmakers and carpenters, 9 music teachers, 2 bookbinders, 5 printers, 10 auctioneers, 8 shipwrights, 1 chemist, 1

A Poverty-Stricken Cadet

Thomas Munro went to India as a cadet in 1779. He rose rapidly through the ranks and later became Governor of Madras. In this letter to his sister, dated 23 January 1789, Munro endeavoured to correct some British misunderstandings about the lifestyle of young officers in the East India Company's army:

I have often wished that you were transported for a few hours to my room, to be cured of your Western notions of Eastern luxury . . . . You seem to think that . . . I never go abroad unless upon an elephant, surrounded with a crowd of slaves – that I am arrayed in silken robes, and that most of my time is spent reclining on a sofa, listening to soft music, while I am fanned by officious pages . . . . But while you rejoice in my imaginary greatness, I am most likely stretched out on a mat, instead of my real couch; and walking in an old coat, and a ragged shirt, in the noonday sun, instead of looking down from my elephant, invested in royal garments. You may not believe me when I tell you, that I never experienced hunger or thirst, fatigue or poverty, till I came to India – that since then, I have frequently met with the first three, and that the last has been my constant companion.

(G.R. Gleig, *The Life of Sir Thomas Munro*, Vol. I, Henry Colburn & Richard Bentley, London, 1830, p. 73)

An English family at dinner under a punkah, *a cooling device.*

carver, 1 gunsmith, 1 engraver, 48 merchants and their 38 clerks, and 30 barristers.

As Calcutta grew in size, many of the Company's servants sought accommodation outside Fort William. The trend towards "living out" did not meet with the approval of the Court of Directors. They feared, not without justification, that young writers and cadets would develop extravagant tastes which would lead them into debt. Those who could afford it, usually the more senior of the Company's employees, lived in a grand manner. Indian influences could be seen occasionally in the houses in which they lived, in the food which they ate and in the manner in which they entertained themselves, but, generally speaking the lifestyle was distinctly English.

House-building was on an elaborate scale. Certain features – verandahs and porches – were borrowed from Indian design, but the style was usually European. With their classical pillars and elegant staircases, the houses gave the impression of Greek temples. New arrivals often described Calcutta as "a city of palaces". Further south, Madras became famous for its shining white plaster (*chunam*) which was made from ground-up sea-shells. Eliza Fay, writing from Madras in 1780, observed:

> **The houses are covered with a sort of shell lime which takes a polish like marble and produces a wonderful effect. I could have fancied myself transported to Italy, so magnificently are they decorated.**
>
> (Eliza Fay, *Original Letters from India*, Thacker, Spink & Co., Calcutta, 1908, p. 121)

Houses were usually of two storeys. The ground floor was used as a warehouse or as storage space. An elegant staircase led up to the first floor, which consisted of a long hall, with dining and living rooms either side and with verandahs front and back. The staircase continued to a balustraded flat roof, where the cool air could be enjoyed in the early hours of the morning and in the evening. Inside, two Indian cooling devices – tatties and punkahs – were employed. Tatties were screens or mats, usually made of cuscus grass, which were fixed to open doors and windows and kept constantly wet. The

European bungalow in Orissa in 1825.

air blowing through them cooled by evaporation. A punkah was a heavy cloth, fixed to a wooden beam and hung from the ceiling, which could be pulled to and fro by a rope to cool the air. Another distinctive type of house was the one-storey bungalow. The word comes from the Hindi *bangala*, literally "of or belonging to Bengal".

The occupants of these houses employed vast armies of Indian servants. The Reverend W. Tennant, who served as a chaplain in India, observed in 1796: "For some time after my arrival I lived with a private family, where the servants of all descriptions amounted to one hundred and five." The numbers of servants were far higher than those employed in comparable country houses in Britain. Low wages made it possible to maintain so many but religion explained why so many had to be maintained. Amongst Hindus, the caste system multiplied the numbers of servants. Members of a particular caste would only

European house in Bengal, by an Indian artist, c. 1796. Note the classical pillars in Greek or Roman style.

Servants at work in the kitchen of a European house. The largest households sometimes employed over 100 servants.

Domestic Servants and Banians

Alexander Mackrabie went to Bengal to become Sheriff of Calcutta, a law officer, in 1774. He stayed at the home of Philip Francis with two other Company servants. In a letter to his friends in Fulham dated January 1775, he described the domestic establishment in the Francis household:

Our household consists of

A *Sircar* [accounts keeper]	A *Khansama* [head-steward]
A *Jemmadar Peon* [head servant]	A *Compradore* [who did the shopping]
A *Jemmadar Hircarrah* [chief messenger]	4 *Mossaulchees* [torch-bearers]
4 *Hircarrahs* [messengers]	12 Bearers [for the palanquin]
2 *Peons* [footmen]	A Tailor
2 *Khedmutgars* [table servants]	A Washer and Ironer
2 *Soontah-Burdars* [mace-bearers]	A *Durwan* [gateman]
2 *Habdars* [stewards]	2 Watchmen
A cook with two mates	A *Mater* [male sweeper]
A Baker and his mate	A *Matranee* [female sweeper]
A Butler and his mate	A Candle Lighter

These are indoors. There are besides

2 Gardeners, 4 *Syces* [grooms], 3 Grass cutters and a Cow and Poultry feeder

Please to observe that these are only Mr Francis' train, and a very moderate one. I have, as a private man, fourteen, officially about eight more. If you add to these about thirty belonging to two gentlemen, who are of our family, and four European servants, you have our whole suite. Count them up, if you please. When I see them all together, they appear innumerable, a legion, an army, and all thieves.

For the due superintendence of these devils . . . we have an endless tribe of *banians*, chief and subordinate, together with their train of clerks, who fill a large room and control, or rather connive [plot together secretly], at each others accounts. We are cheated in every article, whether of the house, the garden, the stable, or our own private expenses . . . . I do most cordially esteem them the greatest rogues on earth. The *banians* of Europeans have been and are the grand cause of all the luxury, extravagance and extortion of the present time, and will ultimately be the ruin of their country.

(India Office Records)

Palanquin with a British officer and his bearers, by an Indian artist, c. 1828. British officials were usually conveyed in this manner; very rarely did they use their own legs.

perform certain functions. Muslim servants would do nothing forbidden by the Qur'an. They would not touch pork and they would not serve alcohol.

The dietary habits of the British in India left much to be desired. They consumed enormous quantities of food and drink. Late eighteenth-century England was noted for its heavy eating. This presumably explains the broad faces and portly waistlines which are depicted in many of the contemporary portraits. Food in India was a mixture of Indian and European tastes. Returning nabobs made curry and rice popular in England. By 1784 curry and rice had become house specialities at many fashionable Piccadilly restaurants in London. The main meal of the day in India was moved from noon or two in the afternoon to seven in the evening. Eliza Fay described the typical fare at Calcutta in 1780:

> A soup, a roast fowl, curry and rice, a mutton pie, a fore-quarter of lamb, a rice pudding, tarts, very good cheese, fresh churned butter, fine bread, excellent Madeira (that is expensive, but eatables are very cheap).
> (Eliza Fay, *Original Letters From India*, Thacker, Spink & Co., Calcutta, 1908, p. 140)

Over-indulgence in food was matched by excessive drinking. Philip Francis's wine book shows that in one month in 1774, his household

The consequences of over-eating? Stringer Lawrence, Commander of the East India Company's army in India, 1748-59. Lawrence, however, lived until the ripe old age of 78.

British officers at a drinking party. Drinking parties invariably lasted until well into the night and sometimes for several days. Excessive drinking was one of the most common causes of ill-health.

Two Views of Calcutta in the Eighteenth Century

The streets are broad; the line of buildings, surrounding two sides of the esplanade of the fort, is magnificent . . . . The general approach to the houses is by a flight of steps, with great projecting porticoes, or surrounded by colonnades or arcades, which give them the appearance of Grecian temples; and indeed every house may be considered as a temple dedicated to hospitality.

(William Hodges, *Travels in India during the years 1780-83*, London, 1793, p. 15)

We know not when Calcutta first got the title "City of Palaces", though last century it was a misnomer in a place having no glass to its houses and few verandahs to shade off the heat . . . drains three feet deep were reservoirs of filth, sending out annually their three hundred and sixty stenches; the receptacle of rotting animals; even human corpses have been known to be two days in the streets, before being taken away by the police, and thrown into the canals.

(Reverend James Long, *Calcutta and Its Neighbourhood: History of Calcutta and Its People from 1690-1857*, Indian Publications, Calcutta, 1974, p. 71)

Calcutta from the river Hooghly. ▽

Calcutta: a view from the bazaar. ▷

consumed 268 bottles of wine, 99 bottles of claret, 75 bottles of Madeira, 74 bottles of porter (beer), 16 bottles of rum, 3 bottles of brandy and 1 bottle of cherry brandy. William Hickey observed that it was "the general custom of Bengal in those days to drink freely and to assemble in numerous parties at each other's houses". His memoirs are littered with references to riotous and drunken dinner parties.

The affluence and extravagance, however, were only one side of domestic life in India. To the newcomer, approaching Calcutta by boat up the river Hooghly, the houses on either side of the bank might well have given the impression of "a city of palaces". But the main town itself presented a different picture. Much of Calcutta's drinking water was taken from a large open pond in the middle of the town. Diseases such as cholera, malaria and typhoid were commonplace. Some of the suggested cures

were bizarre. They included bleeding and the application of red-hot irons. Dr Ives, a surgeon, suggested chewing rhubarb as a preventive measure. No one knew until the nineteenth century that water had anything to do with cholera, or that mosquitoes were malaria-carriers. The Bengal Council observed in 1780 that the roads of Calcutta were in "a ruinous state", being full of ruts and holes. "It is necessary," the Council continued, "for the convenience and for the preservation of the health of the inhabitants of the said settlement, that the stagnant water should by proper drains and channels be drained from the said settlement, and the filth, dirt and rubbish removed therefrom". Crime was rampant. European vagrants were just as much responsible as the Indian underworld.

The squalor and the climate, together with excessive eating and drinking, eventually took their toll. Letters home from India are littered with complaints about the heat, insects and constant stomach illness. People drank more because the water was so foul. Claret was even recommended for medicinal purposes. William Hickey, when stricken with cholera, was advised to drink as much claret as he liked. No one realized that heavy drinking caused inflammation of the liver. The clothes people wore added to their discomfort. At the beginning of the seventeenth century, Indian clothes – loose cotton shirts and pyjamas (trousers) – were worn for coolness and comfort. But by the end of the century, with the inhabitants of Calcutta trying to imitate fashionable London society, clothes became more formal and less suitable. English black broadcloth and full evening dress came back into fashion, even for large dinner parties when the heat was usually intense. Given these circumstances, it is perhaps not surprising that mortality rates were so high. "Two monsoons are the life of a man", ran a contemporary saying in Bombay. Between 1707 and 1775, of 645 civil servants appointed to Bengal, 368 – 57 per cent – died in India.

The social life of the British in India was similar to their domestic life. It represented a mixture of European and Indian ways, with the former becoming more pronounced towards the end of the eighteenth century as British society began to take root.

A cock fight, painting by John Zoffany, 1792.

A tiger hunt, painting by John Zoffany, 1795.

which were held to celebrate the arrival of ladies from England at Calcutta. These parties were arranged by the leading ladies of the town, and the new arrivals sat up in a drawing room for two or three nights in succession while the whole town flocked to see them. By the end of the century, as more polite means of making introductions were devised, sitting-up parties disappeared. William Hickey in his memoirs condemned them as "foolish and disagreeable", while another observer compared them with "the exhibition of a cargo of slaves". The other principal forms of indoor entertainment were

As in Britain, the rhythm of social life was seasonal. During the late autumn and winter months in England, the gentry flocked to their town houses in London while Parliament was in session. The winter season was one long round of social engagements – dinner parties, theatre visits, dances and gala evenings. Throughout the summer and early autumn the gentry retreated to their estates and country houses. The pattern was the same in Bengal during the second half of the eighteenth century. India's climate followed an annual cycle of three distinct seasons: cold weather, when it was never particularly cold, between October and March; hot weather, when it was usually unbearably hot, between April and September; and the rains, or monsoon, which were sandwiched between the two. The wealthier inhabitants of Calcutta spent the cold weather in their town houses and the hot weather and the rainy season up-country in their bungalows and garden-house retreats.

Social entertainments were similar to those pursued in Britain. Dinner parties were commonplace. The guests delighted in flicking bread pellets about the table – a curious form of behaviour but one which was apparently quite acceptable at aristocratic dinner parties. Quite distinctive of India were the "sitting-up" parties, gambling, during which vast sums of money changed hands, musical evenings and concerts, and the theatre. A Calcutta theatre was built in 1775. The scenery was furnished from England under the supervision of David Garrick, a famous actor from the Theatre Royal in Drury Lane.

As well as the more leisurely pursuit of the evening carriage drive, outdoor recreations included horse-racing and cricket. A Bengal Jockey Club was established in 1808 and the *Bengal Gazette*, one of the early newspapers, records a cricket match as early as December 1780. The main outdoor pursuits, however, were

shooting and game-hunting. With forests and jungles harbouring tigers, buffaloes and wild boar, India became the game-hunter's paradise. Equally popular among the lower ranks were animal fights, particularly bear-baiting and cock fights.

Of the entertainments borrowed from the Indian environment, two became particularly popular. One was smoking the *hookah*, described in a contemporary account as "a most curious machine for smoking tobacco through water, the smoke being conveyed by a tube of amazing length, which is called a snake and is

entertainment borrowed from their Indian surroundings was the *nautch* – Indian dancing. The English became almost addicted to the *nautch*. It was similar to attending the ballet, the difference being that in India the troop always came to a private house. Alexander Mackrabie recorded in his journal in November 1775:

Last night I supped at the house of a Gentleman

Hookahbardar *with* hookah.

A British officer watching a nautch *and smoking a* hookah. *Note the officer's Indian dress.*

washed with rosewater". William Hickey disliked the *hookah* but was told by a friend: "You might as well be out of the world as out of fashion, and it is impossible to get on without it." Warren Hastings sent out dinner invitations requesting guests to bring their *hookahs* and their *hookahbardars* (the servants who looked after the *hookahs*) with them. Even the ladies indulged. The other

40

who has been two months persuading me to
see a Girl dance. You have heard and read of
the Indian Dancing Girls . . . . There was one
Principal Girl who has a thousand Graceful
Airs and a deal of Expression. I could discover
some plan in her operation. Her Gesture well
adapted to the Tones of her Voice.
(*Mackrabie Journal*, November 1775, India Office
Records, p. 141)

The *nautch* was also a recognized form of
entertainment when the Indian aristocracy, the
nawabs and *maharajas*, received European
guests. On such occasions, lavish meals were
provided, together with animal fights and hunting
expeditions. Finally, it is perhaps worth noting
that much later, in the nineteenth century, polo
and snooker were introduced into Britain from
India.

The British recorded their impressions of India in their letters home or in their published memoirs. For many, however, paintings were the best record. Paintings and sketches were rated amongst their most valuable possessions. In some cases, the British themselves were gifted amateurs. Sketching and drawing were desirable accomplishments for the upper and middle classes. For those in the military who were destined to become engineers and surveyors, sketching and drawing were part of their training. Many newcomers, therefore, knew how to draw. Given the long hours of leisure, particularly for the ladies, they had ample scope to experiment with their talents.

As well as amateurs, there were professional artists, both British and Indian. Between 1770 and 1825, some 30 professional British painters and over 20 miniaturists were lured to India by the prospect of fame and fortune. The late eighteenth century was the beginning of the "Romantic" period in European art. The exotic and the

Scenes of village life, by an Indian artist, c. 1770. Note the semi-European landscape designed to appeal to European artistic tastes and styles.

picturesque were in great demand. In satisfying this contemporary appetite, the more successful British painters in India – men such as Tilly Kettle, John Zoffany, George Chinery and Thomas and William Daniell – made significant contributions to the development of British art.

Indian artists were not difficult to commission. As the Mughal Empire went into decline, Indian artists, who were once kept busy at the imperial court, sought fresh outlets for their talents. They were willing to work for foreigners. The Indian style of painting did not at first satisfy British tastes. It was thought to lack perspective and a sense of proportion. Indian artists, however, were noted for being meticulous and painstaking. As they became more familiar with the work of the British artists, they acquired the necessary European style. The result was a new school of "Company Painting" – an attempt by Indian artists to adjust their styles to British needs and to paint subjects of British appeal. Their favourite subjects were costumes, trades, crafts, modes of transport and temples. Equally popular were their natural history drawings. As in the case of the British artists, their paintings also illustrate many aspects of British social and domestic life.

Shawl embroiderer, by an Indian artist, c. 1798. Scenes of costumes, trades and crafts were particularly popular with the British in India.

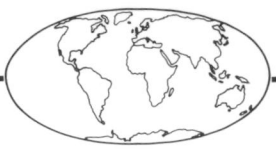

6 "When West Meets East"

The issue of race relations during the British period in India has always been a controversial subject. The eighteenth century has attracted two schools of opinion. One maintains that this was a golden age when the British and Indians met as friends and equals with none of the prejudice and arrogance which became so evident on the British side during the nineteenth century. The other takes a more practical view and argues that the restrictions which existed on both sides were

The Ganges at Benares, a watercolour by Thomas Daniell, c. 1788. The river Ganges is Hinduism's most important place of pilgrimage. The waters are said to wash away sins, and most Hindus try to bathe in the river at least once in their lifetime. One section along the water is also a cremation ground. Many Hindus would like to die near the Ganges, or at least have their ashes scattered in the river.

sufficient to persuade the two communities to keep their distance from one another. There is something to be said for both views but rather more for the second.

A number of British individuals developed a keen interest in the culture, languages and religions of India. The results of their enquiries are examined in Chapter 7. But this interest did not, of itself, create a sense of friendship and equality. As we have seen in their domestic and social life, the British displayed a "Little England" mentality. They adapted to their new surroundings but tried to make them as English as possible.

On the Indian side, the Hindus had long been accustomed to foreign invasions and to living under alien rule. The sight of foreigners in their midst was, therefore, nothing new. But in a society which was divided into a multitude of castes and in which religion was a way of life, the Hindus

could not mix freely or easily. Foreigners were expected to observe their own customs and not to interfere with the customs of others. Hinduism was, and is, one of the world's more tolerant religions, but within Hindu society many social barriers existed. Cantu Babu, the *banian* of Warren Hastings, was a good example of this tendency. Although he worked closely with Europeans in a business sense, he kept himself socially aloof from them. The only concession he made to Western influences was to wear a pair of spectacles.

With the Muslims, or more specifically, the Muslim aristocracy, British relations were sometimes closer. Muslim taboos on pork and alcohol did not prevent social contact. But generally, as Muslim power in India went into decline and the authority of the Mughal Emperor ran over an ever decreasing area, the British attitude changed from one of awe and respect to one of scorn and disdain. Moreover, towards Muslims, there was always an undercurrent of European hostility, which went back to the days of the Crusades of the eleventh and thirteenth centuries when the Christians set out to defeat the Muslim "infidels". What most Western historical accounts over the centuries have completely ignored is the fact that much of the cruelty and destruction during the Crusades was carried out by those fighting under the Christian banner.

Colour prejudice certainly existed on the British side. It was customary to refer to Indians as "blacks", in a tone which was usually insulting. In some cases a number of individuals surprised themselves when they arrived in India to find that they did not feel repelled by the sight of skin different in colour to their own. This of course implies that they went out to India with the preconceived idea that they would be prejudiced in this respect. Colour prejudice apart, the British were invariably critical of their servants, accusing them of being rogues and villains. But the most deeply rooted British prejudices were to be seen in their attitudes towards Hinduism. Hindu temples and festivals were fascinating in their own way but to uneducated British eyes Hinduism represented little more than idol-worship. Moreover, certain Hindu religious rites aroused horror and revulsion. None did so more than *sati*, the burning of widows on the funeral pyres of their husbands. Meaning "devoted", *sati* was supposed to be a voluntary act whereby the widow rejoined her god-husband through the flames of purity. In

British Opinions of Indians

A traveller in a new country observes everything with interest, but of course the objects most interesting to him are the inhabitants . . . . They differed of course from the inhabitants of Europe but scarcely less from those which I expected to see in India. I did not, indeed, expect to find a resemblance to the grotesque representations which I had seen on the London stage; but neither was I prepared for such a total absence of all barbarity and coarseness, for complexions which had nothing repulsive, for features and limbs as delicate as those of women, and manners as gentle.
(Thomas Twining, a writer, quoted in William H.G. Twining, ed., *Thomas Twining: Travels in India a Hundred Years Ago*, James R. Osgood, Mcilvanie & Co., London 1893, p. 56)

The Hindoo appears a being nearly limited to mere animal functions . . . with no higher intellect than a dog, an elephant, or a monkey, might be supposed to be capable of attaining.
(Lord Hastings, Governor-General 1813-23, quoted in Marchioness of Bute, ed., *Private Journal of the Marquess of Hastings*, Vol. I, Saunders & Otley, London, 1858, p. 30)

Sati scene, by an Indian artist, c. 1800. Sati was not sanctioned by the Hindu scriptures and it was not widely practised.

practice it was usually forced upon her by relatives who were either anxious for the prestige of a *sati* in the family, greedy for her possessions, or simply wanting one less mouth to feed. *Sati* represented a corrupt form of Hinduism. It was an ancient custom but not one that was sanctioned in the *Vedas*, the oldest Hindu scriptures. Nor was it widely practised, being restricted mainly to the highest castes.

With fewer recorded accounts, it is not so easy to determine what Indians thought of the British. Such evidence as exists, however, suggests that Indians considered Europeans, not just the British, to be self-interested, arrogant and proud. The exploits of the European "vagabond" or "adventurer" class certainly created an unfavourable impression. They consisted of ex-soldiers and sailors who became tavern- or punch-house keepers, small shopkeepers, European servants who set up on their own and even convicts from the Australian colonies. Many arrived in India without the necessary Company licence. They were a source of considerable embarrassment to the government and the cause of much ill-feeling. In 1792 an English magistrate at Dacca urged the Bengal government to take action "to prevent these low Europeans traversing the country in the manner they now do, by which means they get into disputes with the inhabitants of villages and the consequences which sometimes ensue generally originate from their own bad conduct". Brawling and drunkenness were the most common offences, but some were far more serious. Punishments were ludicrously lenient, the most severe being deportation to England. It was not until 1799 that a punch-house keeper named William Smith, who barricaded himself in on being ordered home and shot a *sepoy* (an Indian soldier in the East India Company's army), was executed for murder. The activities of these vagrants certainly made life difficult for the handful of European missionaries working in India. A chaplain was taken aback when told by an Indian: "Christian religion! Devil religion! Christian much drink, much do wrong, much beat, much abuse others." And when Christian Frederick Swartz, a German missionary in south India, explained to a Hindu dancing girl that no wicked and unholy person would be allowed to enter the kingdom of heaven, he was told in reply: "Alas sir, in that case hardly any European will ever enter it."

In one area of domestic life, however, relations between the British and Indians were extremely intimate. British men were in the habit of setting up *zenanas* (harems) and living with Indian women. These women were known as *bibis*, Indian wives. Formal marriages were rare but men and women lived together as husband and wife, having children and raising families. They were, in fact, married in all but name. The beauty of Indian women no doubt turned a considerable number of British male heads, but this was not the reason for these attachments. The explanation was much more practical.

Very few of the Company's servants went out to India with wives. Writers and cadets were, after all, mere boys. It was not easy for them to return to Britain to marry at a later date. To do this they

---

Indian Opinions of the Europeans and English

The Hindus call all the Europeans in India by the name of *Farangis*, a designation so low, so disgraceful in their tongue, that there is nothing in ours which could reproduce it. As they hold the *Farangis* to be vile and abominable, they have persuaded themselves that these people have no polite manners, that they are wanting in ordered life, and very dirty.
(Niccolao Manucci, a Venetian traveller, tr. William Irvine, *Storio do Mogor, or Mogul India 1653-1708*, Vol. 3, John Murray, London, 1907, p. 73)

Such is the aversion which the English openly show for the company of natives, and such the disdain which they betray for them, that no love, and no coalition [agreement] can take root between the conquerors and the conquered . . . the very reverse is actually taking place, so we may rest assured that the distresses of the people, and the depopulation and desertion of the land, will go hand in hand.
(Seid Gholam Hossein Khan, an Indian nobleman, *The Seir Mutaqherin, or Review of Modern Times, Being a History of India 1706-1783*, Vol. 3, R. Cambray & Co., Calcutta, 1903, pp. 161-2)

had to resign, give up their pay and position, and then seek re-employment. But the prospects of marriage in India were equally remote. Between 1757 and 1800, 2626 writers and cadets were appointed to Bengal. In the same period, only 339 civilian and military officials married in India – about one in eight.

One possible explanation for the low marriage rates is that there were so few European women in India. At any one time during the second half of the eighteenth century there were scarcely more than 250 in Bengal. The young men clearly missed their company. The entry for 18 March 1774 in Alexander Mackrabie's diary reads:

> Evening at the Assembly. Very little company. Judge Le Maistre has a large party at his House to commemorate his Wedding Day. What a plague it is to us, that we must lose our Ladies and our Music.
> (India Office Records)

But numbers alone did not account for the low marriage rates. Matches were sometimes made at the "sitting-up" parties but invariably the ladies did not find themselves pursued by prospective husbands. Some returned to Britain as spinsters. In November 1775 Philip Francis wrote to Lady Clive:

> Among other Calamaties incident to the climate, would you believe that all the Beauty we brought with us has not produced a single Marriage . . . . I believe we must prohibit the further Importation of spinsters until we have disposed of the Stock in hand.
> (Indian Office Records)

The reason for this apparent contradiction – women in short supply but very few marriages – was an economic one. Marriage with a young woman from Britain was so expensive that few of the Company's servants could afford it. Wives required carriages, dressmakers, hairdressers, ladies' maids and nannies. Any children had to be sent to school in England, the mother usually accompanying them. Captain Thomas Williamson, who went to Bengal as a cadet in 1778 and who retired as a captain in 1796, estimated the cost of keeping a wife in India at £300 per year and the cost of sending one child to England at £150. He also estimated that a single man needed at least £600 per year to maintain himself. Until increased salaries were awarded at the end of

---

The Cost of Maintaining an Indian Wife

In regard to the expenses attendant upon concubinage [keeping a mistress] in the East, they will depend greatly upon the circumstances, and the disposition of the gentleman, generally speaking; though, after a while, the lady commonly gains a kind of ascendancy, and goes beyond these limits, which, in almost every case, are marked out by previous contract. A certain sum to be paid monthly; the pay of two, or three, female attendants; an allowance for beetle, tobacco (it is very rarely they *chew* it), shoes, clothes, and *gynahs* (i.e. gold and silver ornaments) are articles in almost every capitulation. Taking a broad outline, we may put down the whole at about forty rupees monthly; equal to sixty pounds sterling per annum; which must certainly be considered no great price for a bosom friend, when compared with the sums laid out upon *some* British damsels; who are not always more scrupulous than those I have described.
(Thomas Williamson, *The East India Vade-Mecum; or Complete Guide to Gentlemen Intended for the Civil, Military, or Naval Service of the Hon. East India Company*, Vol. I, Black, Parry, and Kingsbury, London, 1810, p. 414)

General William Palmer

Perhaps the most famous case of an Englishman living with Indian women was that of General William Palmer, private and military secretary to Warren Hastings. Palmer had two *bibis*, both *begums*, Muslim princesses. The first, *begum* Faiz Baksh, was a member of the Mughal royal house at Delhi. The second was a princess from the state of Oudh. With *begum* Faiz Baksh, to whom he was married under Muslim law, Palmer had six children, four boys and two girls. An unfinished oil painting in 1786 by Francesco Renaldi depicts Palmer, his two *bibis*, two of his sons, one of his daughters and three female attendants.

William Palmer and family, by Francesco Renaldi, 1786. Palmer's marriage was one of the few to become socially acceptable.

the century, few of the Company's servants could afford to get married.

To maintain an Indian mistress, or mistresses, was, according to Williamson, much more convenient, for the simple reason that it was cheaper. In 1810 Williamson published a guide, based on his experience of over 20 years in Bengal, for newcomers to India. Not only did he oppose the idea of sending young ladies from Britain to India; he also argued the economic case for keeping a harem of Indian mistresses. In his guide, Williamson explained that most mistresses were Muslims, a yet further indication that there was more social intercourse with Muslims than with Hindus. Hindu mistresses, however, were not unknown. They were usually of low caste. It was indeed common for British men to live with several Indian women. Philip Francis, with a wife, five daughters and a son in England, admitted in a letter in 1776 that he was living with "Black ladies without end". John Shore, another member of the Bengal Council, who later became Governor-General, likewise had a wife in England and a harem in India.

The British regarded these attachments as a practical convenience, but with rare exceptions they were not socially acceptable. *Bibis* were seldom invited to participate in the social life of the British community. Anglo-Indian children presented problems of their own. In religion and education they were brought up to be British.

Fathers who could afford it sent their sons to school in England and they sometimes made provision for their children and *bibis* in their wills. These, however, were isolated cases. Men in the army who were killed in action left widows and orphans. Many more simply abandoned their families. At the end of the eighteenth century military orphanages were established in India. The boys were taught various trades and the girls prepared for a life in domestic service. The decision to reserve the more senior positions in the Company's civilian and military service for those of exclusive European descent meant that Anglo-Indians were disqualified from all but the more menial tasks. In the army, Anglo-Indians could be recruited only as fifers, drummers, bandsmen and farriers. Prestige and colour prejudice explained this policy of discrimination. An expanding British administration in India could not be seen to be run by people of mixed descent. Anglo-Indian soldiers in the East India Company's army were forced to resign. They transferred their services to the armed forces of the Indian princely states. Some, like James Skinner, won fame and distinction. But, again, these were isolated cases. Anglo-Indians, of whom there were about 20,000 in Bengal alone by the 1830s, carried with them the stigma of illegitimacy. They were shunned by the colour-prejudiced British and treated as outcasts of low social origin by the majority of Indians.

James Skinner

James Skinner, who spent his childhood with an Indian mother, became a victim of the East India Company decree which barred Anglo-Indians from military service with Company troops. In 1795, at the age of 17, he joined the Maratha army. Eight years later, when war broke out against the British, he was dismissed because of his former connections with the East India Company. Reluctant at first to join the colour-prejudiced British in battle against the Marathas, he was eventually persuaded to accept command of irregular cavalry serving with the Company's forces. His troopers fought with distinction but were discharged at the end of the war, the normal treatment handed out to mercenaries. Skinner, however, was no ordinary mercenary. He became known to Indians as "Sikander Sahib", meaning in Hindi "Alexander the Great". The legendary Greek ruler had led an army which reached as far as the north-west frontier of India in 325 BC. Alexander's name had become part of Indian folklore and "Sikander Sahib" could also be translated as "Great Ruler". Skinner raised his own cavalry regiment – Skinner's Horse, or the "Yellow Boys" because of the colour of their uniforms. Skinner's Horse became part of the Indian army and its most honoured cavalry regiment. Skinner himself straddled two worlds. His household was Indian and he was more fluent in Persian than he was in English. But he became a Christian and erected a church at Delhi in honour of his father. When he died in 1841 he was given a funeral with full British military honours.

Lieutenant-Colonel James Skinner. A victim of British colour prejudice, Skinner was one of the few Anglo-Indians to make a name for himself and to gain the respect of both the British and the Indians.

Skinner's "Yellow Boys".

Resaidar Sheik Junnah Hoosein.   Resaldar Gholam Hoosein.   Summud Khan (Nizam Buridar)   Jemadar Abdul Rahman.   Jemadar Mirza Behtomar   Beg

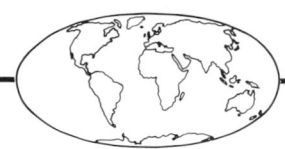

7 British Attitudes towards India

So far this book has argued that the British in India made few concessions to their new surroundings. They ate Indian food and occasionally wore Indian clothes. They enjoyed certain aspects of the outdoor life. A number of Indian words, such as "bungalow", "pyjamas" and "verandah", became part of the English language. Englishmen lived with Indian women because they could not afford to marry European women. But the overall picture is one of the British trying to recreate in India the elegant home and social life of the upper classes in Britain. They hated certain aspects of life in India, particularly the climate and the endless bouts of illness which, of course, in large part, they brought upon themselves. They tolerated life in India because it seemed to be a land of opportunity. They could make money quickly and then retire to a life of comfort in the country they always regarded as home.

There were, however, exceptions to this general rule which seemed to judge India solely in terms of profit. Some of the East India Company's servants were men of great intellect and learning. To these men, India represented a challenge. They were known as the Orientalists. They set out to understand India on its own terms and not to judge it by Western or European standards. Their enquiries enriched European knowledge. For the first time, Europe became aware of the antiquity of Indian civilization. Their work also encouraged a number of Indian intellectuals, like Rammohan Roy, to take a renewed interest in the history and culture of their own country.

Warren Hastings was a great patron of Oriental

Rammohan Roy 1772-1833
Rammohan Roy was a Hindu intellectual from Bengal. He wrote and spoke in Bengali, Sanskrit, Arabic and English. Much of his written work was about religion and in 1828 he founded the Brahmo Samaj, a religious society which believed in the ultimate unity of all religions. A firm patriot, Roy believed that India should adopt Western innovations to her own ends. He welcomed the adoption of English as a teaching language. He was also an active social reformer, campaigning in particular for the abolition of *sati*. He travelled to Britain in 1830 as a representative of the Mughal Emperor. He died in Britain in 1833 and is buried near Bristol, a symbol of the overlap of the history of Britain and India.

Rammohan Roy became a great celebrity when he visited England in 1831. He arrived in Liverpool and stopped in Manchester on his way to London. He visited a number of factories in Manchester, where the workers thought he was royalty. Contemporary accounts speak of the workers crowding round him and calling him "The King of Ingee".

learning. A formidable scholar in his own right, Hastings learned to speak Urdu and Persian, which gave him his taste for Islamic art and literature. He became an enthusiastic collector of paintings and manuscripts. Hastings also suggested that a professorship in Persian should be established at Oxford University, arguing that a study of "the manners of the various inhabitants of the earth, cannot fail to open our minds and to inspire us".

The most famous Orientalist was Sir William Jones, who went to Calcutta in 1783 as a judge of the Supreme Court. Already interested in things Oriental, Jones gathered together all those people he could find with a similar enthusiasm for India. In 1784 he founded the Asiatic Society of Bengal and gave it the task of investigating all aspects of Indian society and culture. A linguist himself, Jones studied Sanskrit, the language in which the Hindu scriptures and literature of ancient India were composed. He translated into English the *Shakuntala*, the masterpiece of India's greatest Sanskrit poet, Kalidasa, who lived in the fifth century A.D. Jones was indebted to Charles

Sir William Jones, founder of the Asiatic Society of Bengal. Jones was the most famous of the Orientalists, men who studied the Indian environment and Indian culture to advance knowledge, not to demonstrate that Western civilization was superior.

Vol. I P 260 RAMA.

Vol. I P 259 CRISHNA

Engravings of the Hindu gods Rama and Crishna (Krishna), illustrating Sir William Jones' paper "On the Gods of Greece, Italy and India", which appeared in the first volume of Asiatic Researches, *Calcutta, 1788.*

Wilkins, a colleague and fellow member of the Asiatic Society, for his knowledge of Sanskrit. Originally a writer who went to Bengal in 1770, Wilkins became the first librarian of the East India Company's library in London in 1801. He was also the first Englishman to gain a thorough grasp of Sanskrit and he translated the *Bhavagad Gita* into English. Meaning "The Song of God", the *Gita* is one of the world's greatest religious poems. It comes from the *Mahabharata*, one of the two Hindu epic poems which were composed somewhere between 300 B.C. and 300 A.D. In the *Gita*, Lord Krishna, who is God, teaches his warrior friend Arjuna about God's power and love.

The interests of Jones and the Orientalists

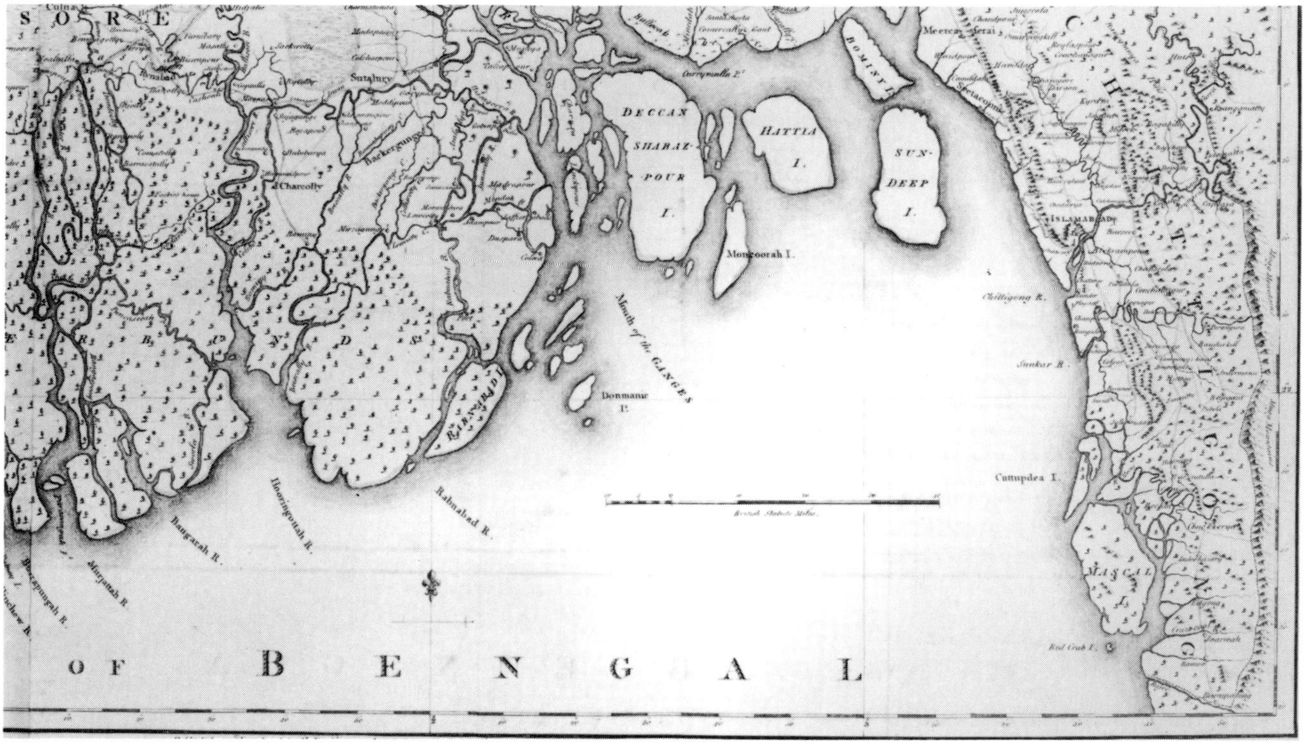

Detail from A Bengal Atlas, *the first of its kind, by James Rennell, October 1788.*

Procession at the Great Temple of Jagannatha at Puri in Orissa, by a draughtsman of Colin Mackenzie, 1818. The Jagannatha Temple is the most spectacular of Hinduism's great temples. Thousands of pilgrims flock to the temple for a festival in June or July.

extended beyond language and religion. They delved into natural history, producing studies of Indian animal and plant life. In 1793 William Roxburgh, one of the Company's medical officers, who had studied botany at Edinburgh University, became the first official Superintendent of the Calcutta Botanical Gardens. Here he began the systematic collection of plants from India. Geographical and topographical surveys of India were conducted by the Company's engineers and surveyors. James Rennell became Surveyor-General of Bengal in 1767 when he was only 21. His survey of Bengal, which took 13 years (1764-77) to complete, was the first of its kind. Subsequently he became a geographer, producing his Bengal Atlas in 1779 and the first approximately correct map of India in 1783. Colin Mackenzie, an engineer, was Surveyor-General of India between 1817 and 1821. Besides his professional interest, Mackenzie had an absorbing interest in the culture of India. His surveys covered not only geography, but also climate, soil, natural history, agriculture, languages, history and the manners and customs of the people. He built up a vast collection of material illustrating these subjects.

Unfortunately, the open minds with which the British pursued their studies of India in the late-eighteenth century did not survive for long. At the beginning of the nineteenth century British attitudes began to change. India was now portrayed as a dead civilization, its people as ignorant and superstitious, and its religion and culture as decadent and immoral. Arrogantly assuming that European culture was infinitely superior, the British began to consider the ways in which they could reform India along Western lines.

One reason for the change was the pressure exerted by missionary societies and the evangelical movement in Britain. From the early days the East India Company had appointed chaplains to minister to the European inhabitants of its own settlements. Missionary activity, however, was frowned upon. The British were a tiny minority in a country of many different races and religions, and the Company believed that it would be dangerous to encourage missionary work. Seeking stability so that trade could flourish, the Company decided to remain neutral on issues which involved Indian religious and social customs. The handful of missionaries in India, therefore, operated without official backing. The most famous was William Carey who went to India in 1793 on behalf of the Baptist Missionary Society. Unable to obtain a Company licence, Carey settled in the Danish settlement of Serampore near Calcutta. Here he established a mission church, which was later followed by a college, and translated the Bible into no less than six Indian languages. Meanwhile, in London, an

John Bull converting the Indians, an illustration from Qui Hi, *a satirical poem published in 1816. The poem attacked many aspects of British life in India and criticized the East India Company for corruption and military oppression. A major point made was British indifference to Indian customs. In this illustration, John Bull is shown as an absentee landlord who, after taking land revenue from the Indians, threatens to force the Bible on the Muslim (seated with hands clasped), the Parsee (standing) and the Hindu Brahmin.*

A Conservative View of India

Our great error in India appears to have been a desire to establish systems founded on general principles . . . that were often in advance of many of the communities for whose benefit they were intended . . . . In our precipitate [hurried] attempts to improve the condition of the people, we have often proceeded without sufficient knowledge . . . . I have been led, by what I have seen, to apprehend as much danger from political as from religious zealots [extremists]. If the latter at times create alarm to the natives from infringing their superstitious observances and religion, the former unsettle their minds by the introduction of principles and forms of administration foreign to their usage . . . . We should proceed with much caution, for the natives never appear to forget that we are strangers . . .

(Sir John Malcolm, Indian administrator, Governor of Bombay 1826-30, giving evidence before a House of Commons Select Committee of Enquiry into the Affairs of the East India Company, 17 April 1832. *Parliamentary Papers*, Vol. XIV, 1831-2, p. 36)

A Utilitarian View of India

In my opinion the best thing for the happiness of the people is, that our government should be nominally, as well as really, extended over those territories; that our own mode of governing should be adopted, and our own people put in charge of the government . . . . The mass of the people, I believe, care very little by what sort of persons they are governed . . . they are equally contented whether their comfort is under rulers with turbans or hats.

(James Mill, Examiner of Correspondence at East India House 1819-36, giving evidence before a House of Commons Select Committee of Enquiry into the affairs of the East India Company, 16 February 1832. *Parliamentary Papers*, Vol. XIV, 1831-32, p. 8)

salvation by faith as the central message of the gospels in the Bible. Members of the Clapham Sect, intellectuals who lived in the Clapham area, had two objectives: to abolish the slave trade and to open up India to missionary activity. One of the members was William Wilberforce, the anti-slave trade campaigner, and another was Charles Grant, three times Chairman of the Court of Directors of the East India Company. The Clapham Sect had considerable influence in Parliament and eventually, in 1813, the East India Company gave way and allowed missionaries to work openly in India.

Pressure for change in India also developed in response to a new political idea in Britain. The idea was known as utilitarianism, which meant the greatest good for the greatest number. The utilitarians were liberals who believed that India could be rescued from its assumed backwardness through the application of Western principles of government, law and economics. Utilitarian thinkers included James Mill and his son, John Stuart Mill, both of whom served at East India House, the headquarters of the East India Company in London. Other utilitarians included Thomas Babington Macaulay, who served in the 1830s as the Law Member of the Governor-General's Council in Bengal. Like the evangelicals, the utilitarians believed that Britain had a moral duty to confer what they regarded as the blessings of Western civilisation on India.

The views of the evangelicals and utilitarians gradually began to dominate British thinking about India during the early part of the nineteenth century. In this new climate, the views of the Orientalists were pushed aside. On matters of policy the Orientalists had been conservative, arguing that Britain should leave well alone and govern where possible in accordance with Indian tradition. It was the utilitarian Macaulay, however, who set the tone for the new reforming outlook. In Bengal he was also Chairman of the Committee of Public Instruction and in this capacity in 1835 he wrote his famous Minute on Education in India. Previously the government had provided modest sums for education to promote studies in Arabic, Persian and Sanskrit. But Macaulay declared that these languages were worthless and argued instead for an educational policy based on the promotion of European literature and science. In consequence, English replaced Persian (the Court language of the Mughals) as the official

evangelical group known as the Clapham Sect began to campaign on behalf of missionaries in India. The evangelicals were members of a Protestant school of thought which believed in

Macaulay's Minute on Education in India, 7 March 1835

I have no knowledge of either Sanskrit or Arabic. But I have done what I could to form a correct estimate of their value. I have read translations of the most celebrated Arabic and Sanskrit works. I have conversed, both here and at home, with men distinguished by their proficiency in the Eastern tongues. I am quite ready to take the Oriental learning at the valuation of the Orientalists themselves. I have never found one among them who could deny that a single shelf of a good European library was worth the whole native literature of India and Arabia. The intrinsic superiority of the Western literature is indeed fully admitted by those members of the Committee who support the Oriental plan of education.

(India Office Records)

language of India and the government set up schools and colleges to promote Western learning in the English language. Simultaneously, Western legal procedures were introduced into Indian law-courts and Western technology was introduced through roads, canals and later railways. A number of Hindu rituals, like *sati*, were suppressed. The British made their presence felt in other ways – fighting wars and annexing princely states to bring still more of India under direct British rule.

It would be quite wrong to assume that the British turned India upside down during the first half of the nineteenth century. Intellectuals in London might debate what the British should do in India but it was far from easy to translate their ideas into practice. The British possessed neither the manpower nor the resources to undertake a major reform of Indian society. Even at the height of British power at the beginning of the twentieth century there were scarcely more than 1300 British civil servants in the whole of India. To speak of British rule in India as if they controlled everything that happened is really a myth. At the heart of Indian society, in the districts and villages, the British were always dependent on local men to perform the day-to-day administrative tasks. Given these circumstances, when we look back to the first half of the nineteenth century, it is hardly surprising that

A sepoy (Indian soldier) in the East India Company's army, by an Indian artist, c. 1800. The refusal of the sepoys at the garrison town of Meerut in Northern India to bite the tips of cartridges which were greased with beef and pork fat acted as the spark for the rebellion in India in 1857.

many aspects of traditional religion and society in India remained untouched. Missionaries laboured away but gained few converts. The British were still inclined to be cautious in certain respects. *Sati*, for instance, was only suppressed because its suppression had the support of Hindu intellectuals, like Rammohan Roy.

It is nonetheless undeniable that the British created a sense of unease in India. Religious leaders felt threatened by missionary activity and Western education. Princes whose states were annexed were pensioned off. Land-holders in the newly conquered territories were dispossessed. Cheap imports of Lancashire cotton goods began to undermine cottage industries in the Indian villages. Grievances such as these are commonly said to have been responsible for the outbreak of

Manifesto of the King of Delhi, 29 September 1857

It is well known to all, that in this age the people of Hindostan, both Hindoos and Mohammedans, are being ruined under the tyranny and oppression of the infidel and treacherous English . . .

Section III. Regarding Public Servants. It is not a secret thing, that under the British government, natives employed in the civil and military services, have little respect, low pay, and no manner of influence, and all the posts of dignity in both departments are exclusively bestowed on Englishmen . . .

Section IV. Regarding Artisans. It is evident that the Europeans, by the introduction of English articles into India, have thrown the weavers, the cotton-dressers, the carpenters, the blacksmiths and the shoemakers etc out of employ . . .

(Quoted in Charles Ball, The History of the Indian Mutiny, Vol. 2, London Printing Company, 1859, pp. 630-2)

rebellion in India in 1857. The rebellion began as a military mutiny when *sepoys* in the East India Company's army refused to use the cartridges for a new Enfield rifle. The cartridges were greased with beef and pork fat, contaminating to Hindus and Muslims respectively. The rebellion has been interpreted as a "War of Independence" but this is going too far. Large areas of India remained passive, even loyal to the British. In Bengal for instance, where Western education was most visible, those who had taken advantage of the new educational opportunities disowned the rebels and supported the government. In September 1857 some of the rebel leaders issued a statement of their grievances in the name of the King of Delhi, Bahadur Shah, the last of the Mughal emperors. But in practice, as subsequent months proved, those leading the revolt were divided over their tactics and aims. The rebellion witnessed acts of great savagery on both sides before it was finally suppressed in 1858. The names of the rebel leaders, such as the *rani* of Jhansi and Nana Sahib, have since passed into Indian folklore as symbols of resistance to foreign rule.

The East India Company was abolished as a result of the rebellion and India was taken under direct British rule. In London, a new Cabinet Minister – the Secretary of State for India – was appointed to head a new government department – the India Office. In India, the Governor-General was given a new title – that of "Viceroy" – to demonstrate that he now ruled as the personal representative of the British monarch. In 1876-7 Queen Victoria was proclaimed "Empress of India" and the British *Raj* was born. The *Raj* was a curious thing. Victoria and her successors had millions of Indian subjects, but in India the British community became even more remote from the Indian people. The rebellion served as a constant reminder to the British of their vulnerability. They constructed their own self-contained world, aided considerably by improving communications which made it possible for them to keep in closer touch with home. After the rebellion of 1858 the British rulers of India put less emphasis on reform and rather more on providing stable government, backed up, of course, by sufficient military strength to protect themselves. They prided themselves on the material improvements they introduced, such as roads, railways and canals. But these improvements were geared to their own

Imperial pomp and circumstance. Lord Curzon, Viceroy of India 1899-1905, arriving in the princely state of Bikaner in Rajputana (now Rajasthan) at the beginning of an official tour.

economic and military needs and not to those of India. In reality, India was exploited. Apart from the question of prestige, India was important to Britain for two reasons: it provided raw materials for British industry and it also provided an inexhaustible supply of men who served in the Indian army. The British used the Indian army to fight colonial wars and to maintain her military influence in various corners of the world. In 1882 Lord Salisbury, a leading British politician, likened India to "an English barrack in the Oriental Seas from which we may draw any number of troops without paying for them".

But not everything changed after the rebellion. Western education continued to develop, with noticeable results. A new class of English-educated Indians emerged. Their education made them familiar with the British system of representative government and they began to campaign for political reforms. In 1885, an Indian National Congress was established to voice their demands. For the first 20 years Congress was a moderate body but it made little headway against the British, who dismissed its members as a privileged minority, not at all representative of the Indian people as a whole. Congress then became more radical and some of its members turned to terrorism. The British responded with repression. Not until Mahatma Gandhi emerged as a nationalist leader at the end of the First World War did Congress develop as a national movement with popular support stretching down to the Indian districts and villages. The Indian masses identified with Gandhi because of his simplistic lifestyle. Gandhi also gave the nationalist movement a new political weapon – non-violent civil disobedience. Major political campaigns were waged under Gandhi's leadership in the 1920s and 1930s but it was the Second World War which finally broke the back of British resistance. By then, the leaders of India's Muslims were determined to have their own independence and so, when the British finally left India in 1947, two new states – India and Pakistan – were created.

Mahatma Gandhi, seen here in August 1947 with some of his followers in conversation with the leaders of the Muslim community in Calcutta. When India became independent and was partitioned in 1947, riots broke out in several areas, including Calcutta, between Hindus and Muslims. In this picture Gandhi is discussing ways of restoring peace with the Muslim leaders. Gandhi urged the Hindus of India to look upon those Muslims who could not join Pakistan as their friends and fellow-countrymen. His efforts to promote peace ultimately cost him his life. He was assassinated by a Hindu extremist in January 1948.

Glossary

banian sometimes *banyan*. A Hindu banker or merchant in Bengal. *Banians* were usually attached as brokers to large Indian business houses and they often worked privately in the same capacity for Europeans. The equivalent in Madras was a *dubash*.

begum a Muslim noblewoman or princess.

brahmin the highest priestly caste among Hindus.

chaperon an escort for a young unmarried lady; usually a married woman.

chintz from the Indian word *chint* meaning "showing patches of different colours". *Chintzes* (plural) were painted and resist-dyed cotton cloths admired by Europeans for their texture and vivid colours.

despatch an official (written) communication relating to public affairs.

East Indiaman sailing ship chartered by the East India Company.

expatriate someone who has left his or her country and settled in another.

evangelical member of a Protestant school of thought which believes that the gospels of the Bible teach salvation by faith, not by good works or by religious ritual.

griffin a newcomer to India; young writers in the East India Company's commercial service and young army cadets were known as griffins until they had been in India a year.

lascar an Indian or Chinese seaman on one of the East India Company's ships.

long-boat a rowing boat carried on a sailing ship.

Mahatma "Great Soul"; title bestowed on Gandhi by the Indian people.

mansabdar the highest civil or military appointment in the imperial service of the Mughal Emperors.

monopoly exclusive possession of the trade in a particular commodity.

monsoon a seasonal wind blowing in the Indian Ocean, from the south-west in summer (the rainy season) and from the north-east in winter.

nautch a dance, similar to a ballet, performed by Indian women.

nawab a Muslim nobleman or prince.

palanquin a box-litter, with a pole projecting in front and behind, which is carried by four to six men.

poop the stern (rear) of a sailing ship, behind the mast and on the highest deck.

Qur'an the book of the revelations to Muhammad; the holy book of Muslims.

Raj a kingdom; the British *Raj* refers to the period of direct British rule in India following the Rebellion of 1857-8, particularly after Queen Victoria had been proclaimed Empress of India in 1876-7.

rajah an Indian ruler or Hindu prince.

rani an Indian queen.

scurvy deficiency disease caused chiefly by the lack of fresh vegetables and fruit.

steerage the steering mechanism of a sailing ship; also that part of a passenger ship allocated to passengers who travel at the cheapest rate.

writer a clerk and the most junior position within the East India Company's commercial service.

Date List

1556-1605 Reign of Mughal Emperor Akbar.

1584-5 Ralph Fitch travels through India, the first Englishman on record to do so.

1599 First subscription raised by London merchants for voyage to East Indies.

1600 East India Company established.

1608-11 William Hawkins represents East India Company at Court of Mughal Emperor Jehangir.

1615-18 Sir Thomas Roe, James I's Ambassador to Jehangir; imperial edict grants East India Company right to establish factories.

1700-1800 Power of Mughals declines, although they still rule in name from Delhi, and numerous independent Indian kingdoms are created. War and anarchy prevail widely. By end of century, after conflicts with French and with Indian Princes, East India Company holds sovereignty over almost whole of India.

1740-8 War of Austrian Succession in Europe; Anglo-French conflicts in India.

1744 Robert Clive arrives in Madras as a writer.

1750 Warren Hastings arrives in Bengal as a writer.

1756-63 Seven Years War in Europe; renewed Anglo-French conflict in India.

1756 Siraj-ud-daula, *nawab* of Bengal, attacks British settlement at Calcutta.

1757 Battle of Plassey gives East India Company mastery of Bengal.

1758-60, 1765-7 Clive serves twice as Governor of Bengal.

1765 Mughal Emperor, Shah Alam, grants *diwani* (right to collect land revenue) of Bengal to East India Company.

1772 Warren Hastings appointed Governor of Bengal.

1773 Regulating Act passed in London; comes into force in following year and Warren Hastings becomes first Governor-General of India (until 1785).

1784 William Pitt's India Act establishes a Board of Control in London to supervise the affairs of the East India Company.

1788-95 Impeachment of Warren Hastings.

1793 Most important positions within East India Company's services in India reserved exclusively for Europeans.

1799 Siege and capture of Tipu Sultan's fortress of Seringapatam; death of Tipu Sultan.

1818 After wars against Marathas, East India Company emerges as strongest political power in India: Mughal Emperor still sits on throne at Delhi but as figurehead only.

1818-57 A number of Western reforms are introduced and the Company's territories in India are expanded by annexation and war.

1824-26 First war against Burma.

1829 Prohibition of *sati*.

1830-3 Rammohan Roy visits England.

1835 Lord Macaulay's Minute on Education in India: beginning of development of Western education; English replaces Persian as official language.

1839-42 First Afghan war.

1845-6 First Sikh war.

1848-9 Second Sikh war; annexation of the Panjab.

1852 Second war against Burma.

1857-8 Rebellion in India; Mughal Emperor deposed.

1858 East India Company abolished; India taken under direct British rule.

1876-7 Queen Victoria proclaimed Empress of India.

1878-80 Second Afghan war.

1885-6 Third Burmese war completes annexation of Burma.

1885 Indian National Congress established.

1906 All-India Muslim League established.

1915 Gandhi returns to India from South Africa.

1919 Amritsar Massacre.

1920-2 First non-cooperation movement.

1930-1 First civil disobedience movement.

1942 Quit India movement.

1947 India and Pakistan become independent.

Book List

Mildred Archer, *Tipoo's Tiger*, HMSO, London, 1959 (A Victoria and Albert Museum publication on the mechanical tiger belonging to Tipu Sultan which is now in the museum. The publication is available from the V & A)

Michael Edwardes, *Ralph Fitch, Elizabethan in India*, Faber and Faber, London, 1972

John Harrison, *Akbar and the Mughal Empire*, Harrap, London, 1974

D. Johnson (ed.), *Clive in India*, Jackdaw No. 52, Jonathan Cape

Denis Judd, *The British Raj*, Wayland Documentary History Series, London, 1972

F.W. Rawding, *The Rebellion in India, 1857*, Cambridge Introduction to the History of Mankind Topic Book, Cambridge University Press, 1977

Tulsai Vatsal, *An Illustrated History of India*, Book 3, Oxford University Press, Bombay 1977

Pratula Vadgama and Hugh Sinclair, *The Rani of Jhansi*, Collins, in association with ILEA, 1974

John Watney, *Clive of India*, Saxon House, D.C. Heath, Farnborough, 1974

Peggy Woodford, *Rise of the Raj*, Midas Books, Speldhurst, 1978

Malcolm Yapp, *The British Raj and Indian Nationalism*, Harrap, London, 1977

For Reference

Stephen Ashton and Penelope Tuson, *The India Office Library and Records: A Brief Guide for Teachers*, India Office Library and Records, London, 1985 (Most of the material used in this book is based on sources available at the India Office Library and Records, which is now a Reference Division of the British Library. The sources include ships' logs, writers' petitions and records of service, maps, records of baptisms, marriages and burials, trade reports and accounts, and a host of material, both manuscript [handwritten] and printed, which narrates what it was like to travel to India and to work and live there in the eighteenth century. The Library also possesses a valuable collection of prints and drawings illustrating the work of both British and Indian artists. Details are available from the Education Service, India Office Library and Records, 197 Blackfriars Road, London SE1 8NG)

Patricia Bahree, *India, Pakistan and Bangladesh: A Handbook for Teachers*, External Division, School of Oriental and African Studies, University of London, 1982

Acknowledgments

The Author and Publishers would like to thank the following for permission to reproduce illustrations: Oxford University Press for the map on page 10 (from C.C. Davies, *An Historical Atlas of the Indian Peninsula*); The Board of Trustees of the Victoria and Albert Museum for Tipu's Tiger on page 15; India Office Library and Records for the remaining illustrations.

Cover Illustrations

The colour print shows Robert Clive receiving the *diwani* of Bengal from Shah Alam, the Mughal Emperor at Allhabad, 12 August 1765 (*India Office Library and Records*); the black and white illustration shows a British officer watching a *nautch* and smoking a *hookah* (*India Office Library and Records*). The figure of the eighteenth-century British merchant was drawn by Nick Theato.